FAVORED NOT FORGOTTEN

EMBRACE THE SEASON, THRIVE IN OBSCURITY, ACTIVATE YOUR PURPOSE

ADAM MCCAIN
SCOTT SILVERII

 Five Stones Press

FOREWORD - JAMI MCCAIN

One of my favorite places in my home is my kitchen table. It's right next to a big picture window with tons of plants just on the other side, and tall shade trees in the background. Even in summers, I can open the windows and hear the sounds of nature (hopefully drowning out the consistent dings of text messages and the clicking sound of my fingers typing as I ferociously answer emails I should have handled days earlier).

The beauty of God's creation somehow makes whatever I'm facing more tolerable. Right now, it's one of those very rare days in Dallas where the weather is simply divine! It's the beginning of fall—the shadows are getting longer, the breezes stronger, and the temperatures are just starting to tease that our triple-digit summer might be coming to a close.

Pumpkins, sweaters, and caramel lattes...this is hands down my favorite time of the year. I wish it could last forever. But in my almost fifty years here on this planet, one thing is always certain—this season soon will end. And in its place will come a cold, harsh, dead winter.

Christmas and New Year's aside, I hate winter. There is nothing green and nothing scurrying around. Just dry, dead leaves and branches. And some days, no amount of coffee can drown out the blues.

When Adam asked me to write the forward for his newest book, *Favored Not Forgotten*, my first thought was, "And why are YOU writing this book?" As a wife, mom, and particularly, a pastor's wife, I think seasons of obscurity come more often than seasons of promotion and glory. But then I read many of the truths he shared; recalling many of the stories that came back in full color, and I remembered the depths of hopelessness I watched him walk through.

I can remember us sitting in his car outside my apartment MANY moons past. We were both so young and hopeful of the bright future that we believed lay ahead. And yet, a cloud had fallen over his dreams. He was being asked to make some very difficult decisions, and, as his then girlfriend, I had no idea the depth of pain he was feeling. No idea the weight of consequences if he made the wrong choice. What if he chose what looked bright and shiny, just to speed up the season of obscurity he was in?

I remember another time, not so long ago, when he went from what many would describe as a career pinnacle to complete obscurity and apparent failure, within a matter of days. The world seemed to literally be collapsing around him.

And then, I watched as he stood, literally and figuratively, in the hope he knew he had--the belief and faith that God was faithful—that, like winter seasons before, this also would pass. And God wasn't done with us yet.

I don't know what season you are in. Maybe the landscape outside the window looks bleak, dark, cold and dead. Maybe you've been in a season of obscurity for a long, long time. But this I know, seasons come to go. And God has a spring in your future!

Love,

Jami

FOREWORD – LEAH SILVERII

When Scott asked me to write a foreword for this book, I have to admit I looked at him like he was crazy. What did I know about obscurity? And then he asked me to share my own story of obscurity, and I asked, "Do women go through seasons of obscurity?" I'm not sure why I thought a wilderness season was gender assigned. When I hear the term, I get images of *Bass Pro Shop* and camping and fishing and roughing it—pretty much all the things I have no desire to experience.

I've always been of the mindset that women just power through. It's what we do. We're wives and mothers and housekeepers and book-keepers and nurses and taxi drivers...We don't have time for obscurity or wandering out in the wilderness. Stuff needs to get done. And Lord knows if we're not there to do it, no one else will take it upon them-selves to finish the task. Does that sound familiar to anyone?

I've been there during Scott's wilderness seasons (we never go through just one), and though I struggled with him, prayed for him, encour-aged him, and did everything I could as a wife to be there for him, it wasn't *my* season to go through.

But what I realized as I read this book was that Scott wasn't singled out in his season of obscurity. All of us have been there. This is a subject that every human on the planet can relate to. And it made me start thinking of my own seasons of obscurity—identifying them—then discovering what God taught me during those seasons. I'm not the same Leah now as I was twenty years ago, and thank God for it!

God gifts us with our own journey and wilderness, so our unique experiences can benefit the Kingdom. Yes! I said *gift!* While our seasons of obscurity don't feel like gifts at the time—and it can sometimes feel like we're being punished or like we're not in alignment with God—that isn't the truth at all. The truth is we need those wilderness seasons to grow and transition and mature into the next period of our lives. I always think of Jeremiah 29:11 when I'm unsure where I'm supposed to be going or I feel like I'm in limbo. God promises us he has a plan and a purpose and future for us. All we have to do is trust him during the storms.

My profession is writing, so you'd think it would be easy to sit down and churn out a foreword for your husband. The difference is that my profession is fiction, and spinning a tale is much easier than digging for the truth—and it's a lot less painful. But this book opened my eyes to recognizing, what I'd considered to be one of the most challenging seasons of my life, was actually my wilderness season.

Part of my testimony is that before we went into ministry, I wrote romance novels. And not the Hallmark kind. It was an incredibly lucrative career that provided abundantly for our family. Scott and I were in the early years of marriage, and both of us were new with our walk with Christ, though we'd both been saved early in our lives.

The more I read the Word, the more we prayed, and the closer my walk became with Christ, I was convicted that the kind of books I was writing were not using my gifts to glorify Him. Basically, when I was in prayer one morning, I heard Him say, *Stop!*

I didn't struggle with the decision. When God convicts you of something, it changes your heart and your behavior. So I told Scott that God told me I needed to stop writing romance novels. He took it rather well considering this was our main source of income. Then we went to church the next Sunday, and the message was on the Sabbath. The pastor asked why we felt the Sabbath was the one Commandment that was okay to break.

I left service that day convicted once again. You see, during my search for fame and fortune and identity, which I had while I was writing romance novels, I also became a workaholic. More books equaled more money. And for someone who grew up in poverty, more money was always the answer.

I prayed about it and thought about the message over the next couple of days, and I also did a little math. And then I went to Scott once more, and I said, "God told me I owed Him some Sabbath days—six month's worth to be exact." I hadn't taken a day off in years.

To give Scott credit, he didn't actually say the words, *"Are you crazy?"* to my face. But I knew he was thinking them. A couple of days before I'd told him God wanted me to stop writing what provided for our family, and then I tell him God told me to take a six-month vacation. It's nuts!

Scott and I rallied from the Word given to me, and we crunched numbers. We'd be fine. Even without writing and without new book releases, past royalties were more than sufficient to live on.

Little did I know that this was the start of my wilderness season, and little did I know that Satan LOVES wilderness seasons. It's when we're most insecure. When we question God. Or when we wonder if God is even listening or there. During these transitions is when Satan likes to slither his way in and tempt you, just like he did when Jesus was in the wilderness for forty days. If Satan can tempt you, then you can't fulfill the purpose and plans God has for you.

I started my six months of Sabbaths with enthusiasm. I didn't know how to rest or enjoy life. But I was going to find out. A week turned into a month, and the royalty sales that had been consistent and steady for years started to dwindle. And then another month passed and they decreased even more. We started eating hot dogs at home and going through Financial Peace University. Another month passed and then another. Until we went from making seven figures a year to making what I'd brought home when I'd been teaching school. It was humiliating and terrifying. Just because your income changes doesn't mean your bills do. We weren't sure we'd be able to keep our house, and we made drastic changes in our lifestyle, selling whatever we could to stay afloat.

Right before the end of the six months was at its end, I received a call from my publisher. I was being given the opportunity to write five more books in a romance series to the tune of a couple of million dollars. Talk about Satan tempting us in the wilderness! That money would have taken care of everything and then some. But it wouldn't have fulfilled the purpose God had for me.

I said no.

This is actually a story that's much longer than one should write in a foreword, but I can tell you that God needed me to be in that place of brokenness—in that place where I no longer knew my identity—and in a place of humility. It's in those moments that we discover our true character and who we're meant to be.

I can also tell you, that through it all, we never stopped tithing, and during a church service one week, I felt like God was telling us to give our thousand dollar emergency fund to the Kingdom. Those of you who've been through Financial Peace University know how precious that thousand dollar lifeline was, especially when it was all we had. But we gave it without fear.

Do you know how amazing our God is? We gave in obedience, and he blessed us a hundredfold. There was money being sent to us from ridiculous places. We'd get random checks in the mail that made no sense…*but God!*

I needed this book. And though I don't know you, you need this book too. Even years after some of the darkest days of my life, I can now look back upon that season and see the blessing that it was. God never stopped providing for our family. And we never lost faith that He would continue to provide for us.

I changed directions in my career and started writing mystery instead of romance after my six months was over. Writing is the gift God gave me, so I continue to do it. But he also gave Scott and I creativity and ideas for other ventures where we could use our gifts to serve Him in ministry. And He blessed us for it.

If you're in a season where you feel hopeless or lost, or maybe you feel like you don't have an identity, I want to encourage you and remind you that God is always faithful. I truly believe that He put this word on Scott and Adam's heart to share specifically with you. Read it. Pray about it. And embrace the wilderness. There are great things on the other side.

Leah Silverii

ENDORSEMENTS FOR FAVORED NOT FORGOTTEN

Favored Not Forgotten is one of the most important books I have read in years. It caused me to see God's plan for my life in completely new and fresh ways. Regardless of your season of life or current circumstances, everyone should read this book! You'll be glad you did.

Dave Willis
Pastor and Author
The Naked Marriage Podcast

Adam McCain and Scott Silverii have laid out one of the greatest truths in the entire Word of God. It is preached on rarely but experienced continually. You cannot know God in depth without going through the wilderness, the place where you're not seen, where no one uses you, where people don't understand you and where the lack of applause is deafening.

Moses spent 80 out of his 120 years in the wilderness. But he delivered 3 million Jews from Egyptian bondage. Jesus spent 30 years in training and only 3 preaching. We spend 3 years in training and 30 in preaching. The price you pay for being in the secluded place with God is rewarded with innumerable treasures in both your character and your accomplishments.

Learn and live these truths. Don't put this book down until you get the point. It will change your life forever. You will have the fragrance of having been with the Most High God.

Larry Titus, President
Kingdom Global Ministries

Favored Not Forgotten is a deeply personal and insightful walk through the wilderness seasons of life. Pastor Adam McCain and Dr. Scott Silverii crafted a unique process for explaining an often-complex practice, while offering insightful experiences benefiting the reader in their own journey through the darkness of obscurity.

We've all struggled through seasons in life where it seemed everyone had abandoned us. Yes, even God; but the reality is, walking through the wilderness is based on Biblical principles. Moses, the Apostle Paul, and even Jesus were prepared for God's anointing by first walking through life's transformational season.

I appreciate Adam and Scott's honest, easy way of sharing practical information, along with their wise reassurance that although we might feel like life is crumbling, it is indeed a preparation for receiving the promises of God. This dynamic, spiritual duo shares the hope we all seek in God's assurance that we are definitely favored and not forgotten.

Rashawn Copeland
Author of Start Where You Are
Co-Founder of I'm So Blessed Daily

After teaching a biblical view of creation for the past forty years, I have learned that the Creator of the universe has a unique way in which He has created man to be a Hero. The personal accounts of Pastor Adam and Dr. Scott are a breath of heavenly insight, which can empower you to unfold your Hero image, representing our Lord and Savior.

The Lord would encourage us to embrace the shadows of our lives while we discover God and grow in His presence. Someday we will emerge with something to say that's worth listening to. Allow God to shape you. We are the clay in the Potter's hand.

There may be things going on in your life today that you don't understand. When you finally get to the place God wants you to be, you'll realize that He has been making you into a vessel he can use, bless, and used to bless others. So allow God to shape you while He is working on you. God is not finished yet. 1 Corinthians 15:51-53

Dr. Dennis Lindsay
President and Executive Officer
Christ for the Nations Institute (CFNI)

God always focuses on our inward man, and those things take time to cultivate. In case you didn't know, He's never in a hurry. In Favored Not Forgotten, we learn to embrace the seasons of life knowing God has never left us. Dr. Scott and Pastor Adam remind us that it's in the little things and lonely places that we prove ourselves capable of big things.

These two men are a gift and a blessing to the body of Christ. Knowing them has made my life better. When I first met Scott, instantly I saw his love for people and how he wants to walk alongside those who are in need of help. Then when you think it can't get any better, I meet his Pastor, Adam McCain, who has an explosion of joy and passion for people.

They are the real deal—two men who passionately love Jesus and want to see lives transformed.This book will bring light into the dark and lonely places.

Juan Martinez
Lead Pastor Get Wrapped Church
Spring, Texas

COPYRIGHT

"Now Moses kept the flock of Jethro his father in law, the priest of Midian: and he led the flock to the backside of the desert, and came to the mountain of God, even to Horeb."

— *EXODUS 3:1*

CONTENTS

INTRODUCTION

Let's get right to the point. We're talking about obscurity.

Sure, obscurity sounds like a strangely horrible thing. It might even seem like an odd subject to dedicate an entire book to, but the reality is, we've all experienced the feeling of being insignificant, abandoned, or anonymous. Sometimes you may feel like it's coming from friends, family, or even God.

If you're willing to admit it, most of us have suffered because of obscurity. Our goal in this book is to walk you through what a wilderness season is as it applies to your own life. We want you to understand the reason for these spiritual seasons—to gain comfort in knowing that they are not dark periods of punishment—and to be confident in accepting that the cycles produce renewed purpose for receiving God's promises.

History is filled with stories of great people who have endured their own wilderness seasons before launching into a new anointing or desired destiny. Of course, we'd all prefer to skip past the struggles and land comfortably on Easy Street, but that's not where the strong are forged.

Wilderness seasons can become tough preparation grounds for receiving God's promises. It's an intensive opportunity for shaking off the bad habits and strongholds that have kept you shackled to a current condition. We're anxious to show you that while these seasons might have brought personal difficulties in the past, they are indeed meant for current and future good.

The significance of obscurity can be as challenging to grasp as the actual definition—it's when nobody knows who you are—situations become too hard or complex for understanding—or the opposite of fame. But for this book's purposes, obscurity might look something like this—retirement, termination, promotion, career change, marriage, parenthood, divorce, death of a spouse, empty nesting, remarriage, blending families, obeying God's call, following your dreams, taking a chance, starting a business, doing something bold, getting old, health challenges, saying "No," or saying "Yes." Any of those sound familiar? Then you know exactly what obscurity is.

The topic of obscurity surfaced unexpectedly as Pastor Adam and I met for the first time while my family was visiting his Texas-based church. During the service, Adam said he was from south Louisiana, and that was enough to have me running down to the front after the final prayer so I could share that our family had recently moved from Cajun Country after I retired as a chief of police. The connection imme-diately opened the door for exchanging testimonies about how we each ended up in the Dallas–Fort Worth area.

As hard as I tried to describe the difficulties faced in my wilderness season that came packaged with a new marriage, blended family, and civilian life after twenty-five years in policing, never in a million years would the word *obscurity* have entered my mind. At the time Adam said it, I must have had the nuttiest expression on my face, because I wasn't sure what he meant.

All I knew was the years prior to our meeting had been the hardest times of my life, and it had left me without the proper perspective within which to frame the challenge of transformational life expe-riences.

Adam's one weird word—obscurity—provided an anchor of under-standing for what I had so recently crawled through. With that single word I began exploring the life application of obscurity. With Adam's mentoring, I also came to the full realization that what I thought was punishment from God was, in reality, a blessing that prepared me for the next season in my life.

But this isn't my story, or Adam's story. This is all our story. This book is because a retired chief of police and a former Bible college president bonded and became friends over one weird word. As our friendship progressed, we openly shared how our respective dry seasons of obscurity affected not only our lives, but also our callings to serve God.

Joining forces to write this book is a natural fit. We understand the patterns of the process, and the purpose for the seasons as they have and will affect you. Our unique backgrounds lend themselves to illustrating that no matter what your age, occupation, education, or predisposition in life, we all share very common experiences as they relate to moving into and out of seasons of obscurity.

So why should you care, and what does this have to do with you? You're probably more familiar with the truths of obscurity than you realize. We're even sure you've already gone through these rough seasons in life, and you will definitely journey through them again.

Examples of obscurity can reach back to childhood, or they can be as current as last week. Obscurity is moving from one season of contentment or complacency and into an atmosphere of uncertainty before the haze of insignificance is lifted. In these seasons, maybe no one knew your name, or worse, no one cared to know. You went from being the boss to being lost in the termination of a career, a childbirth, or struggling with the death of a loved one. Maybe your experience was more of a spiritual journey of faith that started with zeal over a calling, but quickly fluttered into the flames of disappointment and unmet expectations.

The details of why we move into these seasons are secondary to understanding what it means in our life and how obscurity will affect our future. Trust us, there is no avoiding it or escaping the shadow of the valley. While it lasted forty days for Jesus and forty years for Moses, there is no timetable to reference. You must recognize why seasons of drought occur, what they are meant for, and what good can come from them.

We want to walk you through the seemingly rugged seasons of dryness and show you the potential that comes as a reward when we remain faithful until fruitful. And because we're both storytellers from the South Louisiana bayou, we'll also have a good time along the way.

One last note before we launch headfirst into demystifying obscurity. Since one of us has decades of police command experience and the other is a lifelong pastor, we first thought the other should take the lead on presenting this information. But after endless rounds of competitive Rock-Paper-Scissors, we agreed that structuring every chapter so we share the details together before carving out our own sections to lend our personal experiences and perspectives would give you a deeper understanding of what it is we're hoping to guide you through.

We want to bring hope to everyone who has found themselves drowning in obscurity—so the light of Christ that first drew you to Him still shines bright, even in the dark.

IDENTIFYING OBSCURITY

WE AGREE the word *obscurity* is odd. It's never really used in a positive light, and without digging into the academic definitions; the word intuitively leaves an uneasy stitch in your spirit. It simply sounds like something we want nothing to do with. Most of the time your intuition is right, except when it involves opportunities for transformational change.

You might notice we have slightly transitioned from speaking of obscurity as a single event, term, or occurrence as if it were a lonely Tuesday night. Instead, we have begun reshaping its application into a cycle of seasons. Also, as we progress, you'll see that this process of setting apart for shaping, refining, and increasing your spiritual giftings is not a one-time event. This is a cyclical phenomenon designed to progress us along the path of our life's trajectory. The Bible talks about being transformed from glory to glory. It is through these periods of transformative obscurity that moving in glory becomes the reality.

But we all, with unveiled face, beholding as in a mirror the glory of the Lord, are being transformed into the same image from glory to glory, just as by the Spirit of the Lord.

— *2 CORINTHIANS 3:18 (NKJV)*

For the purpose of this book and as it applies in your life, it is more realistic to lay a foundation of undefined periods of sustained time rather than one moment. Why? Because the course of your life involves contentment, change, growth, newly defined contentment, different change, unexpected growth, a resistance to leave contentment, fight against change, and unrecognized growth.

This cycle is called life, and whether or not you want it to happen, it will, as we have no choice in the matter. Maybe you were the king of middle school tetherball, but life's cycle moved you beyond that season and into sophomore classes. Hanging with your buds was the best, but dating and marriage became your new goal in life. Then after you'd just gotten the hang of being married, things got twisted up and confused by the birth of kids. The dream job you wanted turned into another career you simply endured to support your family. The golden years you waited for in retirement resulted in part-time work to pay for insurance premiums. Maybe even the spouse you said you would live with forever is prematurely gone.

You see, the trajectory of your life changes. No matter how strong, rich, or stubborn you are, things are going to change. You can either swing off the back of the train's caboose by your fingernails, sit in the coach car as it sweeps and swooshes along rickety tracks to unknown destinations, or you can take your place in the conductor's cabin while keeping a clear vision of where you are heading.

Obscurity in and of itself serves little purpose for edifying the person. Entire seasons of obscurity without purpose, vision, or guidance may actually lead to serious issues of melancholy, loneliness, depression, and potentially suicide ideation. The sense of being disconnected from social, occupational, and familial circles brings feelings of intense isolation.

Often, we find ourselves alone and without the facts to explain or self-justify why we are mysteriously out of the picture and without control of certain areas in our lives. Honestly, while most of us do not expect the universe to revolve around us, almost all of us hope that at the very least, our own lives revolve around our own selves. It doesn't mean we are selfish, but it does mean we prefer to make sure our needs are met.

We are an inherently inward-looking and self-reliant society. This natural rebellion against a reliance on God leaves us unsettled when we find ourselves in a season of obscurity without warning. Whether we are spiritually connected to Christ or simply have a feeling of well-being in our own abilities, experiencing the loss of connection to something bigger than ourselves becomes a stressful and frightening occasion. This is what obscurity leads us into, by stripping away what we once relied upon as tangible safety anchors for how we naturally identified ourselves. In this season of spiritual uncertainty, we refuse to lean into God and instead grasp at the air for answers that aren't available or wait on responses that will not reply. The feeling of being abandoned or irrelevant attacks our very core need for love, security, and significance.

Let's start talking about obscurity in tangible terms. Walking through real-life examples of what seasons of obscurity might look like will help you identify particular occurrences that left you feeling out in the dark. While it's near impossible to list every occasion that signals an entrance into the wilderness, we felt kicking it off with some of the common-occurrence illustrations would facilitate the process. Although, as we put on our thinking caps and assumed our list would implode into a who's who of horribly dark experiences, we were caught off guard by so many seemingly positive circumstances.

Intuitively we thought it would be impossible for a job promotion or marriage to send us spiraling into a wilderness season. How about the joyous occasion of your child's birth, or the pride of your spouse earning a college degree, or walking into the golden years of retirement?

Oddly enough, we've both experienced exactly how lonely it was at the top of our respective careers, thanks to generous and well-intentioned job promotions. Maybe the most common season of obscurity we all face is the double-edged sword of obeying God's call for our life, yet finding ourselves feeling alone, abandoned, and betrayed by the very God who promised us He would never leave us or forsake us.

Been there? Yep, so have we. The truth is, it happens, and we can tumble into the darkness of obscurity. But the light of Christ never stops shining. We will cover this in greater detail a little later on, so hold on to that question or thought.

Not every positive thing in life is followed by a season of obscurity. In fact, most of those good things were a result of having moved through a prior dry period.

Before we move into our personal breakout sessions, we want to put the pieces of what we have covered so far together, so that you will begin to see the big picture more clearly. Feeling obscure can become a negative position within which to find yourself. No one wants the burden of feeling alone, unwanted, and unloved.

The tricky thing about most of our seasons of obscurity is that those feelings exist only within your perception of the times. While it sounds doom and gloom, there is a higher purpose and a brighter light in the darkness. God is with you through each season, and transformation is His goal. This is not your license to surrender because you feel confused or resentful. You are actually on the verge of a major break-through in moving from glory to glory, so hang in there.

If your battle is a spiritual one, then quitting is exactly what the devil wants you to do. See, his only job is to kill, steal, and destroy. He's never created anything, and he can't because creation is outside of his nature. He's locked into actions only within who and what he is—the destroyer. He lies in his attack to destroy your relationship with the Father. Making you think God has abandoned you in the wilderness is a perfect tactic to launch during what is actually a growth opportunity.

Why else do you think that when we first start stumbling into our season of obscurity we cry out in despair, "Father, why have You forsaken me?" Or something to the effect that you feel either God has caused the darkness or has abandoned you within that sightless mist. Satan wants to isolate you to devour you, but we're not going to allow that to happen, are we?

Submit yourselves, then, to God. Resist the devil, and he will flee from you.

— *JAMES 4:7 (NIV)*

It may be hard to accept thus far, but obscurity will be your avenue for true personal and spiritual change. Speaking of incredible change, obscurity is also a form of the resurrection story. You die inside yourself within your own life, you remain buried for a short while, and then you return with a new anointing.

But in reality, who wants to consider being buried, even if for a little while, as a good thing? Well, if you were a seed, that would signal the start of a tremendous growth cycle in your life. Our microwave society wants to skip to the top and then skim along the surface without ever experiencing what might be below. It's actually in the separation we experience when feeling "below" life's surface that the true nutrients for change are found. Don't think so? Toss a seed onto cement and tell us how miraculous its life cycle was.

Now, plant that same seed deep in the dirt and you've got yourself an environment where growth and change begin immediately. You see, finding yourself beneath what you once enjoyed as normal doesn't mean your potential for a new anointing has ended. It's in the only place it is allowed to begin.

God's regular illustrations of seeds, planting, harvesting, and all things horticultural are perfect by design, and although we are not as agrarian a society as we once were, the points are still made. And for the agriculturally challenged, we like to self-describe our faith and kingdom stature in terms of trees. Just remember, it first requires the tiny, simple seed buried in that obscure dirt to become the mighty oak of faith. Let's break down this scripture to look at the beauty of obscurity from a horticultural perspective:

> They are like trees planted along the riverbank, bearing fruit each season. Their leaves never wither, and they prosper in all they do.
>
> — PSALM 1:3 (CSB)

When we feel buried beneath life's surface and alone, but our seeds are planted by riverbanks, or flowing water, we are being nourished by God's anointing. Plants located near rivers are not dependent upon any external sources in the atmosphere to nourish them to grow. The living water has all they need as long as they remain firmly planted below in the rich earth.

The promise of God is that we will bear fruit in each season. Isn't it incredible that even in our seemingly lowest, least productive time of life that He promises we shall produce fruit all year long? How many plants do you know that produce summer fruit, fall fruit, winter fruit, and spring fruit? There are no such plants. And, because you waited patiently out of the way in what may have felt like a grave, you emerge more productive than ever.

Trees with leaves that wither do so as a survival resource measure. It's similar to the way your body prepares itself in the fight or flight stage that pools the blood in your core and leaves your extremities lacking. Trees do the same thing by conserving water and nutrients during the fall and winter. Once it's concentrated at the core, the leaves and branches become brittle and die. But because you allowed for the time buried in obscurity while being fed by the river's ever-flowing stream, your leaves will always be fed and refreshed to support the fruit in every season.

Let's take a good look at the last part of this eternal promise. Not only did you not confuse being buried with being dead, but when you broke through the surface and back into the light, you grew with the power of a new anointing. Thanks to that vibrant identity in Christ you are nourished, always producing, solid even to the furthest tips of your reach, and you will prosper in all that you do. Not in some of what you do, but in all that you do.

Why? Because you are in the Father's living stream, producing Christ fruit, emboldened by the Holy Spirit's sustainment and deeply rooted in the soil of God's promises. The soil is the very same dirt you were once buried beneath, but what might have been mistaken for a grave was indeed God's harvest in the making.

Here's another truth. God is also committed to acting within His nature. He is light, so never ever could He or would He be the source of your darkness. God also adores you like crazy and only wants the best for His loved ones. Speaking of love and adoration, how about we move over into our personal breakout sessions so we can share our insights and experiences with those who we love and adore the most—*you*.

ADAM'S BREAKOUT

I was sitting in our spare bedroom that my wife, Jami, and I had converted into my ministerial office. In silence while staring at the wall, the words "What have I done?" exploded from the depths of my soul.

A year earlier I had relinquished my position as the director of a historic Bible school that trained thousands of students yearly, and at the same time I shut down my international traveling ministry to church plant. In obedience to a prophetic download, my family and I threw caution to the wind and went for it.

I guess I figured that since I was obedient to God's calling, He would yield His favor. On my own, I had translated God's favor as great influence. Why wouldn't I? God had always favored me. Our history together had always been one of obedience and favor. He would ask me to do something radical, and I would obey. And just like that, God would bless my obedience with supernatural breakthrough, excitement, and influence.

But for the first time in my life, there was no breakthrough, no excitement, and no influence. Gone were the lunch appointments with the who's who in Christendom. Gone were the opportunities to influence thousands at a time. Gone were the greenroom moments of mentorship from the heroes of the faith. Gone was the fulfillment of doing big things for Jesus.

I knew planting a local church from scratch with local people would mean sacrifice, but I didn't realize how much I identified with the national and international circles of influence I'd been living within for so many years. In that moment, in my quiet, local office, I was keenly aware of the lack of influence I now had.

For my personal sacrifice of obedience, I dreamed of God rewarding me with a new, more powerful influence to change thousands upon thousands of lives. I envisioned our tribe making such a powerful impact that it garnered the attention of local, state, and national leadership. Instead of self-defined victory, I found myself facing my greatest fear. I was a nobody, accomplishing nothing.

Terror had stricken me that life moved on without me. I was no longer needed, and worst of all, God Himself had forgotten me. I began to view the season of what was supposed to be an incredible church planting experience as instead, some sort of punishment. Surely, I had committed some egregious sin that caused God to remove His favor from me.

He let me wallow in that place of foolishness for months before responding to me. "Adam," He said, "all have sinned and fallen short of my glory. My favor on your life is not the result of your goodness or your badness".

So, if it wasn't my sin that was holding back God's favor then it must have been someone on my team. Can you imagine the next few weeks of me asking God to reveal the culprit, until finally, He spoke to me again. "Adam, I had Judas on my team and I still healed the sick, raised the dead, and fulfilled my purpose."

Understanding that it wasn't my team's fault, my suspicions drove me even further into self-doubt. Still struggling to figure it out on my own, I accepted the fact that there had to be only one reasonable conclusion: Somewhere, I had made a wrong turn. I went left when God expected me to go right, and now, I was at the wrong location. That had to be the reason; otherwise, I would have been mightily blessed.

Over the next months, I gnawed over every life decision made. In the end, all that it left me with was destruction. Still, I was someone who figured things out and solved other people's problems. Yet I was helpless on my own. The more I struggled to find the answer for myself, the more consumed I became with heading toward a mental breakdown. I had always pursued life with fervor and confidence, but now I was running away, hiding from the tough decisions, and apathetic toward every relationship.

Then, like a whisper in the wind, I began to sense the Lord's voice. It was in those moments of being still to listen that the Savior began to set me free. You see, I needed a doctrine adjustment. My entire relationship with Jesus had been built on a merit system. My tit-for-tat belief was that if I did good for Him then He would do good for me. My self-worth was wrapped up in how God used me to do big things. I feared being common. I believed that contentment was an excuse to live below one's true purpose. I had not made a wrong turn. It was God's favor that brought me to this place, the place of obscurity.

God began to deliver me from my flawed system of merit when I understood that He didn't trade favors, that isn't His currency. He began to impart truths deeper than I'd ever known because I had become a vessel capable of receiving those truths. You see, Jesus loves me not because I'm good or bad, but because I am His. I don't have to perform for His favor; I have His favor because I am His child. It's more important, what He's doing in me, than what He's doing through me. What I perceived as me being forgotten was actually me being favored.

SCOTT'S BREAKOUT

To me, obscurity is best described when I look back and remember that 1976 night like it was yesterday. I smile now like I smiled then. The movie theater in my small south Louisiana town featured a low-budget action flick on a lazy Friday night.

The rowdy bunch of pre-teen ruffians, whom I called friends, and I bolted from that rickety old neighborhood movie house throwing roundhouse kicks and windmill uppercuts against the humid night air. The theme song to *Rocky* hummed throughout the pitted parking lot while some kids waited for their folks to pick them up and others hopped on their bikes to pedal home before curfew.

I sprinted along with my crew between parking lot lights until we reached the Pizza Hut catty-corner from the theater. We were too excited to go home. Besides, I had nickels in my pocket for the payphone to dial my folks. We all had found our calling. We were going to become boxers. Better yet, we were going to become Rocky Balboa.

Sure, we were bummed he had lost to Apollo Creed, but that didn't diminish our complete adoration for the Italian Stallion. It wasn't even the excitement of a big battle beneath the bright lights in his hometown of Philly that captivated us.

It was the way he trained for the fight of his life. We'd never seen anyone drink raw eggs from a glass, chase chickens in the street, or run miles in the early morning hours. We were eleven years old after all, but still, the gray sweat suit and fingerless black gloves didn't look like anything we owned. We enjoyed the fantasy of it all.

Rocky was lean, mean, raw, and real. More raw than anything we had ever seen, and every boy at that red-and-white checker-clothed table wanted to be just like him. We all pledged to start our training the next day.

Yep, the theme from *Rocky*, formerly known as "Gonna Fly Now," still buzzed in my ears along with a big-eyed-cat brass-bell alarm clock. Saturdays were usually reserved for morning cartoons and the donuts my dad would pick up from the city bakery. Nope. Not anymore. My mornings belonged to training like Rocky. I was going to be a boxer.

I cracked two raw eggs over the edge of an old coffee cup and a smile etched across my face as the slimy yolk took its time oozing down the sides of the mug. Wisely, I decided to hold off on the egg-drinking until I returned from my run. I sprinted out the door just before the sun peeked over the sugarcane fields or my folks knew I was a new man in training.

I wasn't but a few heavy steps onto the gravel roadway before I realized that what I was doing was nothing like the movie. The theme song faded fast beneath the gasping pants for desperate breaths of thick, damp air, and the lack of blood to my over-exhausted brain lost sight of what Mickey looked like as he spurred his warrior onward the night before in that semi-air-conditioned theater. No, this was real life, and it wasn't as glamorous as Rocky made running before sunup seem.

Where were the city steps, the hordes of adoring neighborhood kids, and the chickens? As I struggled around the block once and peeled off sweat-drenched clothes before getting to the back door of our house, I wondered what happened. I might have also wondered where the donuts and milk were.

What was so appealing about Rocky anyway?

From the vantage point of almost forty-five years later I think I might have finally found the answer. No, it wasn't the bright lights and potential of a big payday for a poor local slugger. It was the movie's focus on Rocky's day-to-day struggle to get by, while also fighting to prepare for a new season in his life.

Win, lose, or draw, the Italian Stallion's life would never be the same after the title shot, but what we were fascinated by, even to this day, was what he was willing to do while no one else was watching. There was no *ESPN* television crew, twenty-four-hour boxing channel coverage, or local newspaper reporters to snipe sound bites. It was him, and only him, in what we now understand to be his season of obscurity.

The truth of *Rocky* is that it was a movie. Actually, it was a lot of movies, and some that probably would have been better off not being made. But for those movies that still stick to our spirit, the most memorable moments were when he found himself alone.

We all want to think that given the same opportunity, we would chase chickens, suck down raw eggs, and smack raw slabs of meat. In reality, we do have our Rocky moments. They come after we've lost a job or a relationship or the realization that we are undereducated or overqualified for our dream job. Our title shots come when our marriage is on the ropes or our kids no longer call.

Maybe as we collapse onto the stool in the corner of the ring with Mickey yelling in our ear that we are not the stud we once were, or that the job market has moved on without us, we realize that *Rocky* is no longer a fantasy, but is now the fight of our life.

It's what we do in those seemingly dark seasons of life that come unexpected and unwanted that add a tangible identification to what we mean by obscurity. Look, Rocky took some serious blows and got knocked down. A lot. But he didn't stay there. What got him back on his feet? It wasn't the lights, camera, and action of fight night. It was the season he spent in obscurity.

Ring! Ring! The bell tolls for you. Let's go, Champ!

2

TRANSFORMATIONAL
OPPORTUNITIES

WHEN WE LISTEN to people talk about being in the midst of a dry season, there is a central theme of feigned optimism choked back by the obvious hopelessness and despair of the unknown. They want to trust God has a plan for them, but times have been so tough that they are struggling to see Him involved at all. Just the fact that they understand what they're going through is obscurity is in and of itself encouraging, except it is usually tough to encourage them. All they know is that while they are drowning, life keeps handing them cups of water.

On the other hand, when we hear people share testimonies about having come through their latest dry season, it's all about what God did for them and how He revealed His will and purpose along every step of the journey. Of course, this joy arises from a hindsight perspective. Their faith and trust in God are renewed and stronger than ever. They rejoice over God's provisions that made paying the mortgage possible or keeping debt collectors away. Amen, and thank you Jesus!

You know the old saying, "If I could go back in time, but still know what I know now?" Well, seasons of obscurity allow us to do that. Moving from old seasons to new seasons while retaining the knowledge and wisdom from every prior phase is a blessing. What makes it uncomfortable is leaving the familiarity of our current season and moving into something foreign. But you do have the benefit of the past to prepare for your future.

Sure, it's a huge shock the first time you find yourself feeling alone and that everything is out of your control but think about how much wiser you'll be. Instead of celebrating the learning opportunities, we tend to associate obscurity with loss of identity, or a threat to our materialistic possessions like finances, career, or personal status in the world.

The truth is, it is usually because of your finances, career, or personal status that you feel like the world is crumbling beneath you. Have you become too fixated on worldly pursuits for God to get your attention? Has He tried to nudge you forward for a while, but you have placed other idols and gods before Him? It's not uncommon to find a place of comfort or even a place where God has directed you to enjoy the provisions for a season, but then it's time to move forward.

God's story of Elijah found in 1 Kings 17 is so relatable in many of these cases where we've become comfortable with life, even if we know we are existing at or below what we know we have been called to do. It's a great read, but in a nutshell, God sent Elijah to an area to be provided for during a severe drought. He would drink from the brook and ravens were instructed to bring him bread and meat twice a day. Not bad, right? Eventually the brook dried up and the ravens were nowhere to be found. God told Elijah to get up and go on to his next assignment for provision. How many of us would have just stayed by an arid riverbed straining our eyes skyward, waiting for the ravens to return like a restaurant waiter?

Why would we do that? Because of comfort in the known and fear of the unknown. Raise your hand if you have lingered a little too long because you were either afraid of what was next or anxiety over not knowing made the current situation more appealing than it actually was.

Maybe it doesn't feel like God is actually doing anything in you. Really, it may feel as though God has completely abandoned you, but there cannot be transformation in you as long as you are holding onto the status quo. Sometimes the truth is, He cannot do anything new in you until He can remove the strongholds in your life that are chaining you in place. And although God has plans to help you prosper and to give you hope, it is still up to you to claim them. Grasping desperately on to the ties that bind you to where you are will not free you to move into where He wants you to be.

It's natural to feel this way, and that is why God uses the supernatural process of obscurity to move us along the path away from the raven-less riverbeds. It is within this benefit of experiencing one season of obscurity that we should begin to understand that it's not an attack against you. Instead, it is a reason to rejoice, because each season is actually providing transformational opportunities.

This is the secret to not only surviving, but also thriving. You may feel like God has put you on ice, when He is actually cooling your jets before activating your anointing. Having your gifts come to fruition is often prompted by a seemingly disconnected action. Jesus the man had an anointing on His life from the very beginning, but His ministry didn't begin until He was about thirty years old. Those first years weren't spent raising the dead and turning water into wine. Instead, they were spent developing physically, spiritually, and acquiring the skills that would be needed to relate to people while sharing His gospel. God's protection in obscurity allowed His anointing to become refined until it was time to activate it with His baptism.

We are an on-demand society, and we want to be wherever it is we will eventually be without waiting, working, toiling, or struggling. We have lost the art of endurance, which only comes through the trials of enduring. Just imagine if a wise young Jesus in the temple at twelve years old had skipped His transformational seasons and was elevated right into His ministry. Do you think a twelve-year-old carpenter's son would be capable of what the thirtyish Jesus endured? How about going to the cross of crucifixion to fulfill His mission of dying for us? No, the reality is seasons of transformation, even when spent in what is perceived as obscurity, are to mature us in our faith and walk.

While most people resent the sense of loss in the wilderness, God uses obscurity to give something to you. He is preparing you for a new season by transforming your life. It might be a new job, relationship, service area, or spiritual gifting. God transforms us in stages of life and experience. We are most familiar with chronological stages of life.

Certain ages bring particular advancements such as crawling, walking, talking, puberty, and a continued trajectory of effects known as "aging."

Non-physical changes include spirit-led development such as coming to know Christ, accepting Him as your Savior, confession, restoration, and spiritual sanctification as we grow in our faith walk. These can occur at any time in a person's life and are transformational phases of life. Concerning your spiritual growth process, transformation occurs not by chronological age but through supernatural maturation. Each phase of new understanding requires that God impart something new in you. And guess where that gifting is imparted? Yep, you guessed it. In seasons of obscurity.

ADAM'S BREAKOUT

I am convinced that humans were not created to produce at high levels nonstop. They need to Sabbath. They need seasons of obscurity. I see three transformational opportunities in obscurity.

1. A time of freedom from the pressure of performance.

If you have ever held a leadership position, then you understand the constant pressure to perform to the level of everyone's expectations. People are counting on you. Failure is not an option. That pressure causes stress, and stress has been the connecting factor to many life-threatening diseases. Obscurity forces you to "de-stress."

My friend and the pastor of the First Baptist Church in my city recently retired. Those last few years seemed to have really taken a toll on him. I noted in our meetings he seldom smiled and seemed to rarely laugh. But just a few weeks into his retirement, I saw him walking in our neighborhood, so of course I stopped to see how he was doing. I called out to him, "Pastor, how's retirement?"

He turned to me with a smile that lit up the sky and replied, "Life is good." We spent the next fifteen minutes laughing and discussing the freedom he was enjoying from the pressures of the pulpit and the cares of the people. What if obscurity is a lifesaving gift from heaven? Just saying.

2. A time to reinvent yourself.

Former President George Bush lives in Dallas, Texas, where I live. Recently, the local news did a special on his newfound passion—painting. Mr. Bush relayed how being out of the "spotlight" had awakened creativity within him that he never really knew was there.

He had spent all of his adult life in business and politics and had never slowed his life down enough to realize his great love for the arts. As the interview went forward it was interesting to watch the young reporter's smugness turn to respect as this great leader described the process of reinventing himself through the arts. George W. invigorated all of us watching as he described the joy and passion he was experiencing by attempting something so far out of his comfort zone. You could see life in his eyes that had not been visible in years. What if obscurity is a gift that can ignite new passions? Just saying.

3. A time to replenish.

From the very beginning of God's relationship with humanity, He worked in a day of rest. He called it Sabbath. Many people misappropriate God's real intention in the Sabbath by seeing it as some religious duty, but nothing could be further from the truth. Imagine if you told all your employees that once a week your company would finance a spa day for each of them? It would be a time of rest, relaxation, and replenishment. During their weekly spa day, each employee would have time with the greatest life coach imaginable with the goal of developing them into the greatest human they could ever become. Every one of them would sign up immediately!

For most of my ministry life, I found I was so busy doing for God that I was losing my relationship with God. There were seasons that I was completely bankrupt, nothing fresh, just recycling old revelations. I validated myself to others by pointing to former successes and trophies of the past. All the while, I was oblivious to the truth that I was void of anything fresh or new. But Jesus was so gracious as He would drag me kicking and screaming into Sabbath seasons of obscurity with Him. He wanted to replenish that which I had used up. What if obscurity is a gift from God to come and let Him personally "Fill your tank?" Just saying.

SCOTT'S BREAKOUT

Have you ever been in a crazy positive flow of life? I had just been confirmed by the city council for another four years as chief of police, with only four years left to a full thirty-year retirement pension. I had a PhD and was teaching college at night when I wasn't traveling the country as an expert in law enforcement and a published author. If you had asked me then, I would have told you that I was at the top of my game, and that in no way could life be any better. Then it happened.

God called me to retire. No way, right? I was doing so much good for others and my work was very important. How could He ask or expect me to walk away at the highest point I had achieved in my career? I prayed, and mostly debated with myself over this for about two weeks. One morning, I woke up and told my wife, Leah, that I didn't want to go back to work. That was the first and only time in almost twenty-six years I had ever spoken those words.

It was clear God had removed the desire for law enforcement from my heart, and after I handed in my two-week resignation, it was over. It was now time to sit back and watch the glory of God begin to elevate me into the high places that an important man like myself deserved to be in the kingdom.

After three months into a well-deserved retirement, there was nothing. I assumed something huge was brewing, and of course, big and important things take time to develop. I waited another six months. Nothing. All the while, I was slipping deeper and deeper into darkness. The identity I'd received because of the badge I wore was no longer there. I was a nobody. I went from being chatted up for thirty minutes while trying to get to my reserved table in restaurants with the people who wanted to know me to not being able to find a seat in Chick-fil-A.

The love and adoration of the public was gone, the security of a regular paycheck and the extra income that came with teaching and keynote speeches had dried up, and the significance of once being labeled the city's top cop had faded into oblivion. I was in obscurity.

Additionally, everything I had been able to conceal behind the badge and the façade of public life was beginning to shove its way to the surface. I had known for years that PTSD was tormenting me, but I had thus far been able to normalize the behavior because I was in a position of authority and operated with minimal personal account-ability.

The depression and bouts of panic I managed to hold at bay behind the badge were now quickly shredding an otherwise calm demeanor. Finally, the need for acceptance and affirmation that I had so easily gained through job performance was no longer a possibility in the isolated world of the retired. I'd spent an entire career rescuing and fixing everyone else's problems, but I was utterly incapable of helping myself.

Little did I know, I was entering into one of the most intensive trans-formational seasons of my life. While still enduring difficulty, my struggles diminished as my reliance on God became more intimate. There was no way I was going to work my way out of the wilderness because I didn't yet have the spiritual skill set required for navigation.

I persevered, and by the end of the first year I had begun to see a light in the darkness. It's weird to think back and try to recall how I knew a shift had occurred. But in that time of despair, I knew exactly when I first saw the light of hope. It was the day I unloaded the same revolver I'd always kept in my dresser drawer for that final day when I would be unable or unwilling to suffer yet another moment. In that moment, I had stopped asking God why and where He was and began to under-stand the wisdom and purpose for the season of obscurity.

Obviously, God didn't need a chief of police in His kingdom, but He did want me, His beloved child. The problem was, even at fifty years old, I had no clue as to who Scott actually was. All I had ever known was that my identity was clearly defined by what I did, and not who I was. I was a cop, and I found security and significance in wearing that badge. It gave me an identity, influence, and acceptance. Once I'd walked away from the façade, I was left with nothing but questions. The biggest of those questions was, "Who am I?"

That is such a complex question for anyone to ask with the expectation of a simple answer. Of course, I knew I was a son of God, but beyond the spiritual realm and into the natural realm of daily realities, our identity consists of a matrix born out of the amalgamation of life's experiences, expectations, education, understandings, and a very personal opinion about who we are based on how we see ourselves. The tricky part about all of this is making sure the assessment is accurate. For someone trained as a precision marksman with a firearm, when it came to my personal identity, I had no degree of accuracy.

As I stopped clinging to and grieving for the loss of who I once saw myself being, I began to gain glimmers of who I really was, and who God wanted me to be. The truth is, and although you may not accept it or be aware of it, God does not punish us. Like any loving father, His joy comes from blessing us. His promise is clearly laid out in *Jeremiah 29:11 (ESV)*:

> *For I know the plans I have for you, declares the Lord, plans for welfare and not for evil, to give you a future and a hope.*

As I moved from the darkness of obscurity and into the light of spirit-led realization, I discovered so much about who I was and even who I wasn't. Honestly, it wasn't easy. Deep hurt from a dysfunctional childhood of abuse came clearly into focus. Forgiving became a theme during this dry season as it was clear I could not move forward while still shackled to my past through soul ties and withholding forgiveness. Setting myself free from the pain, shame, and guilt was so instrumental in exiting my wilderness season, that everything else in life became secondary to healing the wounds from a chaotic past.

Transformational opportunities offer us the avenue to change lanes by addressing past issues, habits, addictions, and misunderstandings based on neglect, absence, or lack of accurate information. The degree of personal change also depends on the individual.

It was like a home demolition and remodeling project. You pull up the carpet to discover tile. Whether or not you choose to keep peeling back the layers is up to you. Breaking tile may eventually lead you to discover the toxicity of asbestos or destruction of termites in your demo phase, and that is the start of reconstructing a rock-solid foundation for your life. But ultimately, it's up to you.

Please be assured that transformational seasons may seem as if you are being punished or abandoned, but God has never once left you. This is a time of blessing you with healing, breaking off strongholds that have and will hold you down, and gifting you with new supernatural skills needed for the next phase in your life's journey. I don't want to over-simplify it with a comparison of a caterpillar to butterfly, but there is a spiritual metamorphosis in your progress. Get ready to spread your wings and fly!

3

COST OF OBSCURITY

THERE IS a cost to everything in life. Sometimes it is associated with money, while other times it may involve consequences. If approached with thoughtful consideration, accurate information, and measured determination, the risks can be minimized to a point where the potential for gain is realized. While that might sound like the lead-up to a hedge fund commercial, the truth is, we regularly find ourselves at the crux of maintaining life's balance.

We love the parable used by Jesus in Luke 14 and the variety of examples He uses to vividly illustrate the point that following Him carries a price. The consequences for fully investing in Christ can cost the very relationships within your earthly family for example, but Jesus doesn't force us to take that action. We have the gift of free will. Of course, there are consequences to our choices.

Jesus continues by encouraging us to analyze the reality of following Him. Can we bear the burden of that price to follow Him, or would we rather cling to the world and its deteriorating possessions and temporary connections? Luke shares how He related an actual counting the cost of following Him to the money required to build a tower, before wrapping up His parable by using war and diplomatic compromise as a teaching opportunity.

For which of you, desiring to build a tower, does not first sit down and count
the cost, whether he has enough to complete it? Otherwise, when he has laid a
foundation and is not able to finish, all who see it begin to mock him, saying,
"This man began to build and was not able to finish."

— LUKE 14:28–30 (ESV)

The point of Luke 14 is to show that we must consider, count, and
commit to making decisions in life if we are going to press toward the
prize. Whether arriving at a crossroads involves hearing the voice of
God or the call of the wild, there are four major areas experienced in
your journey. Recognizing each can help you to maintain a proper
posture, even in the midst of obscurity's darkest grip.

After analyzing all the potential dynamics associated with moving into
and through the seasons of obscurity, patterns of commonality begin to
emerge. It soon becomes obvious that what started as a wide range of
points, that include everything from fear to elation, find themselves at
home in one of four categories we've identified as COST—Calling—
Obscurity—Stabilization—Transformation.

CALLING

This is where it all begins. Unfortunately, this is also where we often
feel like it has ended. It's not uncommon to get lost in the haze of the
band's blast with the deafening silence of misunderstanding. The
calling can also be likened to the wedding versus the marriage. Too
many of us see both as the destination when in fact the wedding is
only the starting pistol.

The cost of following your calling occurs at so many different levels
that it is impossible to address them all, but it is vital to understand
that while it might be difficult to quit a job for more education, or leave
a life of comfort for foreign missions work, the calling is where this
adventure begins.

There is an encounter with God that is undeniable. To accept that
encounter there must be a posture of obedience to the call. This season
is a gift from God, and He will not force it upon you. Therefore, when
we become aware of the calling, the only way to activate the fresh

anointing is through your act of obedience. In that encounter we receive a vision or a word from Him about our state of current affairs and direction for moving forward. It would be so great if in these encounters God provided us with an itinerary. Great, yes, but in reality, it's not going to happen.

It's in this atmosphere of ambivalence where faith and fear collide. Unless you have been given temple instructions like Moses or construction blueprints like Noah, most of our communication within the stream of the Holy Spirit remains a bit mysterious. There is enough detail there to launch drastic life-changing events, but not always a long-term plan for sustainability.

This is where the excitement of hearing a word from God gets mired in the trepidation of questions soon to follow. This is also the perfect time to pump the brakes and assure that it is in fact God's word that's about to send you rushing into a brand-new direction in life. Honestly, there is not much worse than stepping out in faith when there was nothing faithful about your decision to step out. It's like volunteering to walk the plank except that you are in an airplane. Check your surroundings!

> *Beloved, do not believe every spirit, but test the spirits to see whether they are from God, for many false prophets have gone out into the world. By this you know the Spirit of God: every spirit that confesses that Jesus Christ has come in the flesh is from God, and every spirit that does not confess Jesus is not from God. This is the spirit of the antichrist, which you heard was coming and now is in the world already.*
>
> — *1 JOHN 4 (ESV)*

The apostle John instructs us to test the spirits to ensure that they are from God. Why? Because even demonic efforts are spiritual, and in the natural realm of man, we have a tendency to hold bias in favor of our carnal desires. To put it bluntly, make sure you are not leaving your job because you are tired of the boss. Claiming God led you to make that move is a lie. Of course, who is the father of lies? Yep, Satan himself. The cardinal rule here is to follow John's advice as well as the additional encouragement found in Thessalonians. It is not that we can't trust the Word of God, but we sadly can't trust ourselves.

Do not quench the Spirit. Do not despise prophecies, but test everything; hold fast what is good.

— *1 THESSALONIANS 5:19–21 (ESV)*

OBSCURITY

Working through the process of comprehending God's wilderness seasons while trying to embrace the positive intention for transformational growth can become daunting. Having just discussed the bipolar experience of His calling, it is possible to lose sight of the purpose of obscurity when we become so mired in the conflict of the call.

Let us take a step back and head outside for a virtual stroll together. We are heading into the vineyard to talk about grapes. If you are completely confused about this field trip that's okay but taking a quick detour might help you to relax and see this from a new perspective so you can actually enjoy the view. We thought the vineyard would make for a great illustration because grapes, wine, and vineyards are used in parables throughout the New Testament.

There is no getting around this, but seasons of obscurity cause us stress. Even if we fully understand that what we are about to go through is for our personal growth, maturity, and new opportunities, it's still taxing. It is like expecting someone to remain calm about calculus. It is surely going to make you smarter, but there is little joy in the process.

Speaking of stress, did you know grapes produce better when placed under stress? In the industry, it is referred to as water relations, and it describes the amount of water as it affects the production of grapes. When we first learned about the stress grapes endure to provide us with delicious fruit, it seemed like a joke. Was someone yelling at the vines or demanding they do better, or telling them they're just not good enough? Talk about stress!

Actually, when water is restricted, it prompts a transformative effect driven by transpiration through stomata in the leaves and green tissue. Negative water potential (stress) causes the vines to draw deeper to receive moisture and nutrients. This "sucking through a straw" response to induced stress provides a higher level of transformation and thus yields greater fruit production and better quality.

The absence of this stress influence allows the vines to regulate the amount of water in response to their environment. When left unattended, the vines absorb too much water and basically become content with poorer hardiness. This is how most of us live life prior to entering into obscurity. We have found a cozy rut in life that has allowed us to move back and forth without much resistance. Maybe it is a relationship, a ministry, a job, or what was once a great adventure that has waxed cold. Peace in a Christian's life is not synonymous with contentment or a lackadaisical lifestyle.

Seasons of obscurity prepare us for the next phase in our life's ministry. If we are going to work within the realities of following Christ, then we must accept that there is a cost to this supernatural association. Part of that cost is transformational change. We moved from being unsaved to eternal salvation the moment we accepted Jesus as our Lord and Savior, so we are familiar with change in the practical daily realm as well as the spirit realm.

A question often asked is why does moving from glory to glory have to involve such seasons of hardship? For starters, let's refer to Jesus's Sermon on the Mount in Matthew 5, and specifically 5:10 (ESV) where He shares that;

> Blessed are those who are persecuted for righteousness' sake, for theirs is the kingdom of heaven.

We aren't called to walk out the days of our lives without persecution for our faith. We are called to be salt of the earth and light of the world, and that does not come naturally and without the stress of change. Just like those tasty grapes, it requires stress to create change. This is not a punishment, but in fact is an opportunity to break off strongholds and sin habits that may be blocking the activation of your anointing.

We resist obscurity because of the perception of a diminished influence or the devaluating of your message. The truth is, you are growing stronger in your faith walk and relationship with God. Leaders are particularly threatened by the potential loss of influence because they equate that influence with their ability to lead. They often miss the value of seasons in irrelevance as an incubator for growing an open heart and humbled spirit. Whatever level you are currently at is not sufficient enough to sustain you at the next level. God imparts us with new gifts of wisdom, patience, endurance, and depth of discernment, among others.

A final consideration about journeying through wilderness seasons is that there are no prescribed times for moving into and out of the cycle. Becoming aware of the approaching season and embracing it for what it actually is makes the time much more palatable. It is actually a manifestation of God delivering on His word of the Promised Land. If we chose to see ourselves as grasshoppers as opposed to the giant killers (Numbers 13:30–33) God ordained us to be, then we may become mired in the rub of dryness. Although we may feel isolated and outside of where we were once comfortable, it is an opportunity to be bold in your expectations of God's promises fulfilled.

> Then Caleb quieted the people before Moses, and said, "Let us go up at once and take possession, for we are well able to overcome it."
>
> But the men who had gone up with him said, "We are not able to go up against the people, for they are stronger than we." And they gave the children of Israel a bad report of the land which they had spied out, saying, "The land through which we have gone as spies is a land that devours its inhabitants, and all the people whom we saw in it are men of great stature. There we saw the giants (the descendants of Anak came from the giants); and we were like grasshoppers in our own sight, and so we were in their sight."
>
> — NUMBERS 13:30–33 (NKJV)

STABILIZATION

There is light at the end of the tunnel, and just before you are able to grab a big old handful of brightness, comes a period of stabilization. Your time in the wilderness has caused you to reconsider so many facets of your life. Most things you assumed were solid and immovable became the most uncertain aspects of all. That is one of the beautiful things about obscurity—you don't know the true you until you have first lost who you thought you truly were.

The value of love, security, significance, and purpose cannot be minimized. They form our deepest needs. We toil in obscurity because we have lost the self-satisfied levels of each of them. We become stable once we have either understood that it is okay to let them go, or they were forced from our grip. In that void of self-satisfaction, we come to Christ either out of desire or despair.

It reminded us of the story of the man who penned the timeless classic "It Is Well With My Soul." Horatio Spafford lost his four daughters when their oceangoing vessel was sunk in an Atlantic collision that left only his wife Anna alive.

On board a ship to meet his grieving wife, the captain pointed out the location where Spafford's little girls had lost their lives. It was aboard that ship Spafford wrote "It Is Well With My Soul." In your season of obscurity, has what you perceived as loss become well with your soul?

When we discuss losing things during our seasons of obscurity, we usually focus on ourselves, but the reality is there are so many more things in life to be lost. It is during these times that we begin questioning the value of worldly things and life as we are presently living it.

Once we come to an understanding that nothing on this earth is permanent, we begin to see God in a different, eternal light. This is the only source where there is hope unending. Becoming stable means accepting the losses from a once-complacent position of influence or comfort. Losing a loved one is certainly a drastic occurrence, but most often we experience levels of loss in those very same needs; love, security, significance, or purpose.

Our identities and location among the social strata are rooted within, not who we are, but what we do for a living. Losing a job or source of income strikes at the core of who we are because we have placed our earning ability above that of God's willingness to provide.

A reduction of earned income threatens our financial security and simultaneously diminishes our assumed stature among peers, friends, and loved ones. The loss of a relationship or friends during this season strikes at the heart of our value as a person, our popularity and our worthiness to be loved. Even the sense of waffling during seasons of uncertainty disrupts our desire for attaching value to our sense of purpose.

This phase of stabilization involves a realization that all because the size of your audience or sphere of influence has shrunk, it does not diminish the quality of your message. This is the time to dig deep and lean into Christ for the boldness to accept this opportunity for transformational change. Remember the parable about shifting sands?

> *Everyone then who hears these words of mine and does them will be like a wise man who built his house on the rock. And the rain fell, and the floods came, and the winds blew and beat on that house, but it did not fall, because it had been founded on the rock. And everyone who hears these words of mine and does not do them will be like a foolish man who built his house on the sand. And the rain fell, and the floods came, and the winds blew and beat against that house, and it fell, and great was the fall of it.*

— *MATTHEW 7:24–27 (ESV)*

There is one major phase remaining, but until you become like the wise man, then nothing God is waiting to bless you with will be sustained in a shaky or pre-obscurity position. The old person must be transformed to receive the new blessings for the light of their next season. But if you are still clinging to the old days and old ways, you will not have the capacity to activate God's new anointing. The following are markers we have identified as clues you might not have let go of your past persona:

1. Telling or reminding everyone who you used to be.
2. Defaulting conversations and thoughts to the good old days.
3. Name-dropping people you once held as important to regain social clout.
4. Trying to re-establish former relationships that feel familiar and legitimize your past.
5. Resistance to meeting new people who don't fit the profile of old acquaintances.

Arriving at the point of being stable in your season of obscurity is also when you first feel like you are beginning to catch traction against circumstances that left you helplessly slipping through uncertain terrain. You are close to experiencing a major breakthrough, so hang in there. No looking back!

> *Let your eyes look directly forward and your gaze be straight before you. Ponder the path of your feet; then all your ways will be sure. Do not swerve to the right or to the left, turn your foot away from evil.*
>
> — *PROVERBS 4:25–27 (ESV)*

TRANSFORMATION

Who you become in this new season of life depends on what anointing God has activated within you. Actualizing the full effect of transformation requires an active acceptance of the gifts God has imparted in you during this time as well as a grateful heart for the strongholds broken off of your life. There can be no spirit-filled transformation (glory to glory) unless you embrace the work God has prepared you for.

It is not uncommon to emerge from a season of obscurity with a tainted heart because of the personal resistance or trauma experienced during the trials. It is also not uncommon to abandon the good works He wants to do in your life because once the trials are over, you simply want to escape from the process and return to what was known or comfortable. God is not going to force His will upon you, so the gift of free will now becomes your blessing or curse. Choose wisely.

How do we know if we have entered into a new season of life that includes God's full transformation? If you refer back to the markers we listed under the Stabilization section and you no longer do those, then it is a great indication you have accomplished the purpose of your most recent wilderness season.

> *Therefore, if anyone is in Christ, the new creation has come: The old has gone, the new is here!*
>
> — 2 CORINTHIANS 5:17 (NIV)

The simplest illustration to share about this phase would be the metamorphosis from caterpillar to butterfly. If God can turn a worm into something as beautifully amazing as a butterfly just think what He will do for you. Trusting in God's promise of Jeremiah 29:11 is vital to having the full assurance that His plans for you do require transformational change, but within that shifting process, it is to ensure you are the better vessel to receive His gifts.

Ancient potters working with clay would often apply wax to their broken vessels and sell them at market. They were not as strong or long lasting as righteously crafted pots, but it wasn't uncommon for unscrupulous merchants to take advantage of shoppers. Wow, things really have not changed much have they? Honest merchants would place signs on their wares that read *sine* (without) and *cera* (wax) to assure customers that their pottery was without blemish. This is believed to be where we get our word *sincere*.

Moving from one phase in your faith walk to the next requires that your vessel be sincere. The transformation phase of your wilderness season is like the kiln or firing process of sealing God's good work in you. Without these phases, the prior you would not have been able to receive the new anointing. Imagine that cracked pot placed over an open fire. The wax probably melted faster than the customer realizing they had been duped.

It is within this transformation phase that you will begin to receive new opportunities in life. It may be a new career or relationship. It might even look like the chance to restore your finances and begin to embrace stewardship as part of living the blessed life. Your new you has been prepared by God the Father, but ultimately it is your choice whether to accept or reject the activation of His anointing. There is a COST to everything in this life and having the light of Christ as your guide ensures that you remain on the right path.

ADAM'S BREAKOUT

CALLING

The rented U-Haul groaned as we inched our way up the last incline between us and our new assignment. Five hundred miles back in the rearview mirror was what used to be our home, our family, our culture, our security, our identity, and the place of God's outpouring on our lives. It was where thousands of young people had called us pastors.

Ahead of us was the great big unknown. What we did know was that our new city had a population larger than our entire former state, but a church smaller than our former youth ministry. We had uprooted and arrived into the great big unknown because God had called us to leave everything we held dear and help a recent upstart church in the metropolis of Dallas–Fort Worth.

The only thing I knew about Texas was that spicy crawfish boils were not a part of their weekly culture, and for a good old Cajun boy like me, that was a hard pill to swallow. It really is the simple things in life. I would also like to tell you my calling into that season of obscurity was beautiful and exciting. Unfortunately, for all of us, it was simply horrible. I was mature enough in my faith to know there could be beauty in the transition, but I was also childish enough to complain to God about how much it "sucked." Especially the way it went down. That's for another time.

OBSCURITY

Upon our arrival in the Dallas–Fort Worth metroplex, the next months showed me a host of experiences that made me aware we were in obscurity. Things like walking through the mall and not recognizing a soul, or eating in a restaurant without one person walking up to us and saying, "Hey, aren't you the McCains?"

I would not necessarily call us Christian celebs, but we definitely had great influence where we were from and a few trophies to show for it. But in Dallas, no one cared. The transition to a new church and a new staff wasn't any easier. Since we were unknown to this team, we felt as though we had to prove ourselves over and over again. There was no honor for our past successes, and that really ticked me off. Starting over was no fun at all. Ever been there?

STABILIZATION

In this initial obscurity cycle I think we stabilized more quickly than in the cycles that were to come. I would attribute that to two things: first, the bridges back to where we came from were pretty much burned. Since there was no glimmer of recovering the former glory, we were freed up to concentrate on what was before us. Only many cycles later did I realize the power of no way back. Second, our new assignment began to take off, and we immediately saw growth. Oh, sure, we didn't have as many resources as before and building from scratch is so laborious, but even with all those obstacles we saw miracles. It was as though God was prospering everything we touched. Looking back now I had no idea how spoiled I was. Many seasonal wilderness cycles later, I recognized God's sweet mercy on that initial obscurity journey, and I thank Him every day for it.

TRANSFORMATION

I didn't notice it at first, but something was happening inside of me. Unbeknownst to me, I had previously become a corporate executive minister. The new assignment and transition forced me back into the trenches, and back to what really mattered, by helping people establish a genuine relationship with their Creator. Ministry was raw and alive again. Since tools were sparse, creativity was alive. Since we came with no relationships, any new ones being established were fun and invigorating. We didn't have much, but we were alive and that was FREEDOM!

SCOTT'S BREAKOUT

I was so confident walking into the mayor's office to hand him my two-week notice. God's calling was crystal clear, and although I thought I would spend the rest of my life in law enforcement, it was the clarity of His call that gave me that degree of confidence. I had been obedient, and now I was prepared to reap the rewards for what I called "trading up."

To be completely honest, my act of obedience was not sacrificial in expectation. I thought if God wanted me to give up my career as a chief of police, my tenure as a college professor, and my lucrative consulting work with the federal government, then surely He was going to amplify my material crowns and earthly gains.

It was weeks after my sudden retirement from policing that the reality of obscurity crept in. Of course, I had no idea what was actually in play, so I resisted the possibility of Him actively being at work in my life. I panicked at first and thought I had made a huge mistake. I even explored the possibility of asking for my job back. Doesn't that sound like the Israelites who'd just been liberated from Egypt's cruel pharaoh?

> They said to Moses, "Is it because there are no graves in Egypt that you have taken us away to die in the wilderness? What have you done to us in bringing us out of Egypt?"

> — EXODUS 14:11 (ESV)

I think it was my initial resistance that led to a longer season of wilderness. I had suffered for years on the job from past personal pain and the effects of occupational PTSD. Without an understanding that I was in an improvement process, the darkness dragged me to the edge of suicide.

I am a little embarrassed to admit it, but I thought He had actually abandoned me. Maybe it was punishment for all of the bad I had done in my life. For a period, I began to accept that reasoning and labeled myself as broken and worthless. I was a doer and a fixer who had spent my life helping everyone else with their problems, but in the pit of my despair, I couldn't save myself. It's what was making the once-unthinkable idea of ending it all seem more plausible.

The question I kept asking was *Why?* Why did I retire? Why did I move our family to Dallas, Texas? Why was my health eroding while I sat sedentary around the house packing on seventy pounds in that first year? And why had God called me to serve Him only to abandon me? But once I had moved into the stabilization phase, those questions were answered with the most perfect response—God.

I began to see God's work in my life. I was being connected to other Christian men who quickly became brothers whom I loved. With each new friendship, I noticed that we all shared the common calling from God to break free from our past chains of pain, shame, and guilt. We were being renewed and transformed for His service, and through their testimonies and mentoring, I began to feel like I was standing on solid ground for the first time in a long time.

Although I felt more stable, I still wasn't sure what God had in store for me. I was, for the first time, enjoying moments of peace and contentment alone and with my wife and family. Our marriage was stronger than it had ever been, and the labels of brokenness I had placed over my life were no longer there. I was stable but still unsure what it all meant for my life.

Honestly, at that point, I didn't care about what might happen next because I had come to understand that peace in life did not mean an absence of chaos. Once I had become stabilized in my faith walk, it was the depth of my roots that kept me grounded in the storm. Experiencing that level of supernatural security was something I had never known but immediately embraced.

That security allowed for God to begin speaking into my life the truths of my past. I carried so much pain from a violent and dysfunctional childhood home that it still held station in my life as an adult. Behaviors I had normalized created constant conflict with my wife and were manifestations from those horrible early experiences. It was as though God was showing me not only what was wrong, but why it was wrong and how to heal from it. Being able to examine the course of my life to grasp the cause, cure, and care for what it was that harmed me, opened the path for significant transformational change.

My season of obscurity made it possible to get away from the worldly trappings that helped me suppress past pains. It was when I thought I had nothing, that I had actually gained everything—me. Finally, it was through the transformative process that I came to know the real me. I had been dominated and lived in fear my entire childhood. I pretended to be someone I was not through college, and law enforcement allowed me to hide what it was that was hurting me to the point of suicide.

All I had ever known or shown to others was a razor-thin façade. It wasn't until the wilderness season that I came to know and love the man who was a child of God. His renovation allowed me to understand why He called me out of law enforcement in the first place. My job was blocking my freedom because it had become a crutch that prevented me from walking in light. I was who that badge said I was instead of who my Father God called me to be.

When it all made complete and total sense was the first morning I was set to preach. As I sat on the front row of the church with Leah, my heart was pounding like crazy in my chest. The senior pastor was introducing me, and I shook with nerves wondering if I was going to be able to walk to the altar to share my sermon.

Suddenly the Holy Spirit asked, "Do you remember the day I called you out?"

I smiled and whispered, "Yes."

The Holy Spirit replied, "It starts today."

See, God didn't want or need a chief of police in His kingdom. He wanted His son to share the story of a life and the victory I now know because of His love and mercy. It was because I came to know the COST involved that I transformed from a career of locking men up to a lifetime of setting them free.

4

OBSCURITY IN THE BIBLE

WHEN WE BEGAN SORTING through the process of life's seasons, the acronym COST became very clear. It overlays with such precision to so many scenarios that we had to continue developing it as an application in this work. As a matter of fact, it not only applied to our lives as it will apply to yours, but we are going to go back thousands of years to show you that what we all go through is no different from what our biblical heroes underwent.

We are going to highlight three of our favorite people from the Bible to give you a deep, foundational appreciation for this ancient phenomenon of the Holy Spirit's work in our lives. Obscurity is not a modern self-help idea that is useful for explaining why we go through tough times. It is as old as time itself, as vital today in shaping your life as it was back then.

To walk this out, we are going to present each of the stages of COST: Calling—Obscurity—Stabilization—Transformation—and then apply practical examples shared from the lives of Moses, Paul, and Jesus. Watching their lives applied to the most current circumstances you may have experienced will help you come full circle, not only in your own lives, but theirs as well.

Each of our three heroes experienced distinct, albeit different, callings into God's service. Moses's activation was a work in progress that expanded over many decades. Paul's entree into kingdom service was completely spontaneous and unexpected, while Jesus's calling was always an inevitable reality though just a matter of time and maturation. We hope in sharing three very different perspectives that you will relate to those areas that speak into your life.

MOSES

CALLING

Moses's calling occurred through various stages and experiences in his life. It was not clear until his encounter on Mount Horeb with the burning bush (Exodus 3) that God had a specific purpose for his life. That experience was the calling that activated Moses's ministry.

He, like most of us, had a deep, spiritual seed planted that pointed him toward a direction of kingdom service. Moses only came to understand that direction after he lived out his transformation through obscurity. It was at that season of life that God's anointing became available for activating the gifts and God's plans for his life.

Do you have a passion for something but are unsure of what it should look like or how to go about getting started? This may be the same early calling Moses had for leading his people to freedom from the bondage of Egyptian oppression.

His calling as a liberator was meant to be activated after his season of elite education in the house of Pharaoh, as well as after his forty years of obscurity as a shepherd of his father-in-law's sheep. When Moses attempted to first activate his role in leading the Israelites, it unwisely resulted in his murdering a cruel taskmaster. God had appointed Moses to lead His people to freedom, but it was not going to be through a violent revolt or insurgence. Their escape from slavery would be to glorify God's way and not Moses's might.

Please don't become impatient if the time between your calling and the realization of God's plan takes longer than you wish. The worst thing you can do is self-activate what you think your calling should be, as opposed to what God has in store for you. Moses killed a man in haste. You may just kill the plans God has for you.

OBSCURITY

We would venture to say that Moses takes the trophy for enduring the longest seasons of obscurity. We usually think of his second forty-year season as he led God's people through the wilderness prior to the nation of Israel entering into the Promised Land, but let's go back. Way back.

Moses's life had been an exercise in obscurity. Separated from his biological family for his own safety, he grew up in the house of Pharaoh. Although he received the world's most advanced education and knew privileges reserved for royalty, he lived in a state of familial dysfunctional obscurity. This season not only left him apart from, but with a deep desire for, his native people. It also created an identity crisis that would bring pain into his life.

It was this deeply rooted personal pain that drew him to help his Israelite family, and ultimately led to the murder of an Egyptian taskmaster. Despite his efforts to help them, the Hebrews rejected Moses and saw him as a threat to their own safety. That rejection in the face of his self-activated calling sent him into a hasty season of obscurity that would last forty years. But it wasn't in vain, because God works all things for good (Romans 8:28) and the good work in Moses began in his first season of obscurity.

We might ask what was the purpose of God allowing Moses to grow up in the refined comfort of the house of Pharaoh only to send him fleeing into the desert as a sojourner for four decades? It was in this season of obscurity that Moses discovered who he was, and where he learned the survival skills of a shepherd that would sustain the exodus of an entire nation. Moses gained the caring, nurturing, and guiding heart of a shepherd instead of the skilled, masterful education of a ruler.

Are you second-guessing what you are experiencing in obscurity? Maybe even doubting that God has called you at all? Keep in mind that you have not yet been shown God's plan for you and therefore are not aware of what skills and gifts you will need to activate that anointing. Remain open and sensitive to the leading of the Holy Spirit so that you don't miss out on one drop of anointing oil you have got coming to bless you.

STABILIZATION

One of the most stabilizing events in Moses's life was the affirmation of his ministry by his father-in-law, Jethro. Because of his dysfunctional family history, Moses never enjoyed a relationship with his father. Pharaoh was a surrogate who only provided commanding expectations, but never personal affirmation.

His God encounter at the burning bush set the stage for clarity of vision, and Jethro's paternal affirmation of his ministry calling set Moses on the solid ground to fully activate his calling. Additionally, the deeper Moses pressed into faith-led action, the closer his walk with God created a stable atmosphere for service.

Have you been on a path of questionable uncertainty? It's common during seasons of obscurity for God to send a Jethro into your life to provide additional support for moving the rest of the way in your journey. Stay alert to the people in your life, as new or existing relationships can emerge in a support, but not a leadership, role. God is your guide and transformational potential is the stabilization you will require to proceed.

TRANSFORMATION

We usually picture Moses in a transformative state as he descends Mount Sinai with the Ten Commandments. His face aglow with the fire of God's glory and his white flowing hair whipping in the wind. Actually, that was Charlton Heston in the movie, but Moses's spiritual conversion occurred even before that glorious moment. It occurred when still fearful and unsure of his own ability that he stood before the powerful pharaoh to demand that he let his people go.

We will know when we have entered into an environment where we once would not have had the discipline to go. It isn't because we are smarter, braver, or now belong there, but simply because God said to go. Sure, we may ask questions before setting out, but the transformational phase occurs once we go despite our questions, doubts, or fears. We go because God said so and, in His word, we are confident in His plan. We become a vessel!

PAUL

CALLING

Coming to know Christ looks very different for different people. For some, it may have been a gentle influence leading to a commitment, and for others, they might have grown up in a Christian environment where a Christ-led life came naturally. Still, for others, their calling to Christ is quick, fast, unexpected, and radical. That describes Paul (Hebrew name Saul) and is what launched him into becoming one of the most influential and enduring disciples of Jesus Christ.

OBSCURITY

Similar to Paul, most major and minor figures in the Holy Scriptures experienced significant wilderness seasons. It almost seems like a "rite of passage." The apostle Paul is an amazing example of someone who entered into and transitioned out of multiple seasons of obscurity. A look at the Book of Acts shows us several examples where he became sharpened for kingdom service. Acts 9 gives us the first of such cycles in his life.

> As he neared Damascus on his journey, suddenly a light from heaven flashed around him. He fell to the ground and heard a voice say to him, "Saul, Saul, why do you persecute me?" "Who are you, Lord?" Saul asked. "I am Jesus, whom you are persecuting," he replied. 6"Now get up and go into the city, and you will be told what you must do."
>
> *— ACTS 9:3–6 (NIV)*

This encounter with Jesus shifted everything in Paul's life. Like many people, Paul's experience with Jesus ignited a radical transformation, but prior to that moment Paul (Hebrew name Saul), had been on a quest to destroy Christianity. Continuing through the passage of Scripture, you will find that in Paul's transformational change, he instead lives only to convert his fellow Pharisees and Sadducees to follow the way of Christ.

As you can imagine, that did not go over very well, and his former friends plotted to kill him. Because he was now a marked man, Christians had to help Paul escape Damascus before he fled to Arabia. It was in a foreign land that Paul spent the next two years in obscurity. It was during this first season of obscurity that Paul developed a deep abiding relationship with Jesus. It was also within that space that his doctrine and value system became redefined.

STABILIZATION

The apostle Paul's final cycle is the one that touches most people the deepest. After years of missionary journeys, church planting, healing the sick, raising the dead, and securing doctrine; the apostle Paul was imprisoned. Those angry Jewish leaders had finally caught up to him.

He spent the next five years in a jail cell or under house arrest. He was taken out of the movement and the movement went on without him. The churches that he planted and the truths that he shared had come under direct attack. His imprisonment thwarted his ability to go and set things right. Eventually, even Paul's closest friends failed to come check on him, and obscurity became a very lonely place.

Paul's stabilization became possible because he had already cycled through the difficult wilderness seasons as God continued to prepare his new anointing to serve Him. It was because he had developed a mature stability, that he was able to press his fight for the kingdom.

TRANSFORMATION

Paul's experience was difficult, and thanks to his being forged by the fire of obscurity did he succeed. Despite the extreme hardships and danger, he understood the purpose of what he had been through and the value for what he would produce. It was during this season that the "Prison Epistles" were written.

Wouldn't it have been easier to waste away and whine over the difficulty of his situation? Sure, but once we have experienced God's preparation process, we can no longer sit idly by.

Despite his most dire circumstances, and while churches planted by the apostle Paul no longer exist and the people he saw healed and raised from the dead have long since gone to heaven, his Holy Spirit-inspired writings, composed while imprisoned, continue ministering to us two thousand years later.

What if some of our finest work is to be done in obscurity, when our perception of influence is at its lowest, when our productivity has slowed to a crawl, when we seem less valuable to others, or when we feel washed up? Even when we feel locked down by life's circumstances, we are always truly free through Christ.

JESUS

CALLING

Talk about having a calling on your life! Jesus's life on this earth was purely because of His calling. His situation was unlike any of the other examples we shared, but it was a calling all the same. Maybe you are one of the fortunate souls who were born to walk in the Spirit from the moment of birth. If you were brought up in a Christ-centered family that instilled the values of God's Word, there will still be seasons of obscurity in life. Why?

Just as Christ was born into His calling, He still had to walk through seasons of wilderness as He grew and matured in both personal experience and spiritual readiness for activating His anointing. Can you imagine the infant or the twelve-year-old Jesus hanging from a tree for our sins? Of course not, and that is why we all must move through seasons following our calling. The calling is simply a first step in the activation of God's purposeful anointing.

OBSCURITY

While the biblical account of Jesus's life gives us glimpses of His birth, exile into Egypt, and as a twelve-year-old boy in the temple, it doesn't mean He was living His early life without purpose. We know He was a carpenter, which meant that His dad, Joseph, taught Him the trade that he used to provide for his family.

We think this is so important to understand because although Jesus the spirit man knew His calling, Jesus the natural man worked hard to learn a craft that would provide for Him just as it did for His dad. Actively engaging with Joseph shows His humanity and desire to learn the craft that would pour skills into His early life that benefited Him once His ministry was activated.

Jesus's first season of obscurity to prepare Him for ministry occurred immediately after He received the power of the Holy Spirit and His Father's affirmation of His identity. Do you see how important affirmation is in seasons of obscurity? Moses received it from Jethro, and once Jesus had His Father's word, His ministry was also set into motion.

> And a voice from heaven said, "This is my Son, whom I love; with him I am well pleased."
>
> — *MATTHEW 3:17 (NIV)*

In a world where we all seek social proof and approval, you might think that hearing God Himself proclaim Jesus's identity would have catapulted Him to the top of His ministry. But this isn't grounded in social media's fickle favoritism. His Son was immediately whisked away into the wilderness for a forty-day season of obscurity.

Mark gives us a brief narrative of His trials. It was necessary for Jesus, within the new identity of His anointing, to experience this obscurity to ensure His readiness was present along with His calling. Remember, He had spent thirty years learning to be a carpenter and moving into His ordained calling would not happen without this opportunity for furthering His reliance on His Father.

> At once the Spirit sent him out into the wilderness, and he was in the wilderness forty days, being tempted by Satan. He was with the wild animals, and angels attended him.
>
> — *MARK 1:12–13 (NIV)*

Even after His baptism and anointing, it still was not time for Jesus to become known. Similar to you having moved based on a calling, it is vital to be patient in revealing to others the work God is doing until the appointed time. Allow obscurity to blanket you in God's protective hedge while He imparts what you will need to excel in the new season of your life. Just as Jesus did not begin an empowered ministry until the Holy Spirit came upon Him, it is the same for your giftings.

The process of you becoming a new vessel requires different phases, and you will begin to gain perspective in stages. Do not rush or resist these progressive steps. Never could Jesus the child have survived Herod without exile, or the cross as a young boy. God protected Him in obscurity as He will protect you, but only if you remain within His grace. Once you begin to feel the old itch to go back to your old ways, or impatient about the journey ahead, take comfort in knowing that because God protects you, He is also keeping you in a safe harbor until you are ready to launch into a new you!

This was serious business for Jesus the Christ, and it should be serious business for you. Our seasons of obscurity are not about having a bad day while waiting for the sun to come out tomorrow. This is about God the creator loving you so deeply that He can't wait to bless you with His gifts.

STABILIZATION

Was there ever a chance for Jesus to fall to the temptation by Satan? While we all give a resounding answer of no way, the reality is, without that potential to fall, there would not have been temptation. Matthew 4:4 clearly states that the Holy Spirit led Jesus into the wilderness to be tempted by the devil. If it was just ceremonial, then Jesus would not have been tested or tempted and Satan's presence was not necessary. Because this was a time of testing and a deeper reliance upon God His Father, Jesus experienced the trials as much in the fully spirit man as He did in the full measure of the natural man.

In and of himself, there was no ability to resist the devil. But in the power of God's Holy Word, Jesus not only resisted the devil, but commanded him away (Matthew 4:10). We must remember as we exit what may have seemed like our darkest days in obscurity and begin to see glimmers of light, that there remain trials and temptations in our path. Satan knew the Scriptures as well as Jesus did, but he was lacking the power of God to activate those timeless words into influence. Remain cautious that as you become stable that your relief for escape does not morph into ego or pride for having come through. Stick close to Christ for discernment and direction for the rest of the way out.

The stabilization of Jesus's wilderness experience and progression into a fully actualized gospel ministry came as the angels attended Him after dispatching Satan from His presence. This is a powerful time and although you might have questioned God's presence in your life, please be assured He has never left you or abandoned you. God will send the resources you require to move from a season of stabilization into the full transformative role He has assigned for you.

> Jesus said to him, "Away from me, Satan! For it is written: 'Worship the Lord your God, and serve him only.'" Then the devil left him, and angels came and attended him.

> — *MATTHEW 4:10–11 (NIV)*

TRANSFORMATION

The transformative process that is part of our seasons of obscurity are giftings designed to increase our faith walk, to reflect more of God in us and to become the suitable vessel for pouring into and pouring out of. Transformation is the full circle that began when God first placed His desire in your heart through a calling to serve. That service comes in many different arenas ranging from pastoral to parenthood.

Next, it continued as you moved into the purifying kiln process of obscurity until cycling around to stabilizing your experience just short of full-fledged transformation.

When Jesus performed His first miracle on the third day at the wedding in Cana (John 2:1–11), it was not about making sure the host had more wine. It was about the completion of God's work in imparting the gift of ministry activation in His son's life.

Once Jesus experienced the full authority through the completion of His transformative process, He was endued with an unlimited authority to walk in the faithful works of God's light.

5

OBSCURING OUR DEEPEST NEEDS

Do you find yourself questioning what it is all about? Like really, does it have to be this difficult to become so blessed? Between raising the kids and studying for the next exam, it's not uncommon to question God about the big picture. It is pretty simple; God created us with a purpose—that purpose is to glorify Him. But to glorify God is not the same as a self-created cheerleading squad. *"Go God!"*

> *Everyone who is called by my name, whom I created for my glory, whom I formed and made.*
>
> — *ISAIAH 43:7 (NKLV)*

The truth is, God did not need us. He does not have an ego to pump or need people to high-five. When you look back over the course of human history, we have pretty much made a mess of things. So when the Bible says to glorify Him, it is only out of His love that we were created, and for love that we remain.

We were created in the image of God, so His thumbprint is in our DNA. Because He is love, then we too are a reflection of that love. It is in the highest form of love that we find the fulfillment of our deepest needs. Yet obscurity often leaves us feeling needy and unloved. Let's explore why.

Then God said, "Let us make mankind in our image, in our likeness..."

— *GENESIS 1:26 (NIV)*

Ask yourself, what exactly are your deepest needs? Beyond things like money, a miracle weight-loss pill, and free cable TV, try pressing deeper into the spiritual realm.

In creating us, God imparted four needs deep into our temple where the Holy Spirit resides. They are safe there and are satisfactorily activated when the Holy Spirit empowers us. When reviewing the course of your life, you'll realize it wasn't until you received the power of the Holy Spirit that you realized the fulfillment of those needs.

On the contrary, life before and apart from God distanced our reliance upon love, security, significance, and purpose. In the state of spiritual separation is when we languish by trying to satisfy those needs with external sources and by our own, limited ability. This is precisely what happened to Adam and Eve. They had every conceivable need met and exceeded.

If you are familiar with Genesis 1, He not only created mankind, but God gave them dominion over everything on earth. He provided for their internal needs of love, security, significance, and purpose. He also provided their physical needs with food and provisions. To put it in today's terms, "They had it good." The only caveat was that they exercise the discipline of respect and restraint by not eating of the fruit from the Tree of Knowledge of Good and Evil.

Once their desires shifted (thanks to temptation) from an internal edification by God to a rebellious character driven through a self-reliant need to seek an external stimulant, it created the separation from God through the breach of their obedient submission upon Him. Ever since that moment, the gulf between mankind and God caused an environment of unfulfilled expectations for self-gratification.

It wasn't until the crucifixion and resurrection of Jesus Christ that the bridge across that gulf was connected through the propitiation of sin.

Additionally, Christ's ascension (Acts 1) provided for the Holy Spirit's arrival for the purpose of activating our anointed relationship with God the Father. Thus, the potential for once again having our deepest needs satisfied by God has been restored through the power of the Holy Spirit residing in our Holy of Holies (1 Corinthians 6:19–20). Let's talk about each of those four needs.

LOVE

> *So we have come to know and to believe the love that God has for us. God is love, and whoever abides in love abides in God, and God abides in him.*
>
> — *1 JOHN 4:16 (ESV)*

Because God is love, the relationship with Him is based on the highest form of love—agape. It is not a tough stretch to understand the concept that God loves us beyond compare, and that through His ultimate love, we can know, experience, and enjoy the satisfaction of being loved.

In seasons of obscurity, we initiate an action in response to His calling. Following that act of faith, there may be times when we are without the emotional or tangible expressions of His love. To put it bluntly, we feel like God has abandoned us. It causes an array of emotions ranging from fear to anger, but the lesson in this is that having His presence in our life shines light on the darkness that creates hurt.

The truth is that never once during our wilderness seasons has God abandoned us. Do you recall the words that the natural man in Jesus cried out as He hung upon that rugged cross?

> *And about the ninth hour Jesus cried out with a loud voice, saying, "Eli, Eli, lema sabachthani?" that is, "My God, my God, why have you forsaken me?"*
>
> — *MATTHEW 27:46 (ESV)*

Why would God's own Son feel abandoned by His Father? The same reason Adam and Eve did and the very same reason we do—sin. While humanity's very first couple committed sin to self-satisfy their deepest needs, and then brought sin to the rest of the human race, Jesus took on the sin of the world (1 John 2:2) so that we might be restored. It was only for that moment when Jesus became the sin of the world that God could not look upon Him, and in that instant of spiritual separation we also know the pain of love's void.

Setting love in its proper perspective relative to one of our four deepest needs, just like Jesus on the cross, there is no joy without it. Obscurity can cause us to feel like love is absent, but the truth is, it was love that sent us into the season—because God loves us.

SECURITY

> *And you will feel secure, because there is hope; you will look around and take your rest in security.*

> — *JOB 11:18 (ESV)*

Where do you find security? Most people we speak with first think about the financial security to provide for their family and then physical security to protect them. Other responses equate a good job with security, along with positive relationships. These are all important on a temporal level, but once we move into a season of obscurity, we discover these anchors might either be the problem in our current situation, or have been diminished, replaced, or severed as we move through obscurity.

Loss, such as a job, marriage, promotion, identity, or financial status are usually instances that proceed, or that occur immediately after we enter into an atmosphere of obscurity. How deep that loss is suffered becomes a tangible measure of how dependent you were upon that item as opposed to God's provision of security.

These seasons involve the breaking off of strongholds that have chained us into the current status of our faith walk. If we are going to experience spiritual breakthrough, then there are gifts and activations of your anointing that must be received through God's gift. The New

Testament warned against pouring new wine into old wineskins (Luke 5:37–39) because the vessel was not capable of containing the substance (blessing).

If God gifted you with a new anointing for the next season of your life without first preparing the vessel to receive that gift, you would not be capable of receiving the new gift into your old vessel. This preparation of the vessel through the sanctification process is where security in Christ reveals you are ready to receive that fresh anointing.

SIGNIFICANCE

> *What do you think? If a man has a hundred sheep, and one of them has gone astray, does he not leave the ninety-nine on the mountains and go in search of the one that went astray?*
>
> — *MATTHEW 18:12 (ESV)*

Tied closely to our materialistic desire for security is significance. External gratification comes through material objects, such as the car we drive or the neighborhood where we live. What college we attended, advanced degrees, or even what church we attend all provide levels of external significance. Professional titles and associations with people of power and influence. Satisfaction from being liked or followed by a social media influencer is often cause for celebration, as well as taking a selfie with a celebrity or professional athlete.

Can you see how fleeting that is for meeting your internal need for significance? If we realized the eternal benefit of being a child of God, we would stop idolizing media props who direct us on everything from what to wear to who to vote for on election day. As a child of God, we are so much more significant than what we drive or what others refer to us in our job. We are kings and priests:

> *And hath made us kings and priests unto God and His Father; to Him be glory and dominion for ever and ever. Amen.*
>
> — *REVELATION 1:6 (KJV)*

In seasons of obscurity, we experience a loss or diminishing levels of significance as provided by outside sources. Retirement that promised to usher in the golden years has devolved into a chaotic time of losing your identity. The joy of motherhood can bring about the guilt of being edged into society's shadows as you are labeled "only a mom," as opposed to the significance you once attached to your career before kids.

When we aim at moving targets, our shots are only as accurate as where the target once was. Social significance is indeed a moving target. The difference between the boss and the assembly line is one bad decision. Your fall from stardom might be a malicious rumor or a misinterpreted social media post.

Instead of constantly fighting to fill your need to feel important, why not give it a rest and become spiritually significant? Obscurity has a way of showing us the fleeting nature of external validation. You'll know it's external validation because it usually means the source pumps our pride with false praise.

Once we are laid bare through the wilderness trial, those very same external satisfiers soon fail to clothe us in the false confidences for believing we are independently sufficient. In God's kingdom, the mark of understanding your place of service, as well as your trajectory through obscurity's cycle, is where you see yourself among others. We will end this section with an example of what it requires to be truly significant.

So the last shall be first, and the first last: for many be called, but few chosen.

— *MATTHEW 20:16 (KJV)*

PURPOSE

For I know the plans I have for you, declares the Lord, plans for welfare and not for evil, to give you a future and a hope.

— *JEREMIAH 29:11 (ESV)*

Purpose is an age-old concept that has mystified those without one and sustained others who have discovered theirs. From pondering the purpose of life to the purpose of going on for another day, we have been confounded by its veiled taunts of combining wishful dreams with tangible results.

Although not scriptural, J. R. R. Tolkien wrote, "Not all those who wander are lost," which seems to give solace to people in the still-searching category. To those of you wandering within your wilderness season, it is absolutely vital to know there is a compass, a path, and a light. Of course, these are all found in Jesus Christ.

It is not uncommon prior to receiving your calling to actually be in a place where you are fully enjoying the fruits of your actualized purpose. The irony of obscurity's process for gifting you with God's new grace is we are usually plunged back into an atmosphere where chaos instead of purposeful intentionality reigns.

Why would God obscure the purpose you came to realize in lieu of a season of uncertainty about your future purpose? Our natural inclination when confronted with something new is to grasp for something old. Spouses return to abusive relationships, addicts relapse into drug abuse, stressed out CEOs ignore doctors' orders to cut back at work, and parents rush maternity/paternity leave to get back to their professions.

Part of our obscurity process requires us to question or completely abandon what we once accepted as our purpose. There is a new purpose in your next season of activated anointing. If we continue to cling on to what once was because we were good at it or it was comfortable, then we remove God's purpose from becoming our purpose. Without that seamless stream of God to man, nothing will be imparted and made to work for good.

Romans 8:28 (NIV) shares biblical truths about purpose:

> *And we know that in all things God works for the good of those who love him, who have been called according to his purpose.*

This supernatural purpose acquisition requires that we love Him and cannot continue in sin with an expectation He will reveal your purpose. Another note from 8:28 in regard to the difficulties we experience in obscurity is that although not all things are good, God will indeed use them for good.

Too often we grow weary in the midst of this process of firing the kiln because we fail to accept there will be tough times in service to His kingdom. These experiences are used to either bring you closer to God or make you more like His son. It is okay to struggle over the initial loss of seeing your life's purpose with vibrant clarity for a season. God will light your path when where you have been is no longer what satisfies your deepest needs.

In those moments when you are searching for the path of purpose, many people wonder if they misunderstood their calling from God; or maybe have unrepentant sin; possibly if someone close to them has sinned, or whether they are not working hard enough. The truth is, it could be one, or all, or even none of these situations. Obscurity in the wilderness is not about punishing you for sin or sloth. The wilderness seasons take time to fully draw out the God within you so that you better reflect His light to others. Here are six things to do for pursuing God's purpose in your life:

- **Pray** – Instead of stumbling around in darkness, ask God for wisdom and direction as directed in James 1:5.
- **Read God's Word** – To hear His voice is to read His Word. It is the most tangible and direct method of communicating with us. Psalm 119:105 assures you that His Word is a lamp to your feet.
- **Identify Gifts and Strengths** – God's purpose is usually associated with things you are already good at. Although He likes to stretch us beyond comfort zones, He has also gifted you with special abilities prior to your obscurity season and uses that to sharpen them.
- **Pursue Passions** –Psalm 37:4 tells us that God gives us the desires of our heart. If you are passionate about something, it is usually because God planted that seed within.
- **Engage Others** – Proverbs instructs that we need guidance. Seeking wise counsel can help reveal your purpose through encouragement or prophetic words spoken over your life.

- **Take Time Out** – Although others around you may be affected by this season of obscurity, make no mistake, this is your journey. Creating time apart to meditate, pray and journal your experiences, questions, and desires is helpful for gaining a peaceful foothold in the process. Hebrews 11:6 promises God will reward those who seek Him.
- **Trust God** – Pursuing purpose can cause worry, fear of loss, and a sense of defeated abandonment, but truly trusting God is part of the progression through this season of obscurity. Psalm 27:14 encourages us to wait upon Him. Trust Him in your patience.

The stripping away of those external factors we rely upon for satisfying our deepest spirit-based needs is similar to most military, first responder, and fitness bootcamps and academies. To create a better version of the person capable of upholding the ideals and requirements of the organization, a process of first breaking down and later building up has to occur.

No one has walked, or will ever walk, in from the civilian streets one day and received the Navy SEALs' trident pin the next day. There is a rigorous process of transformational change and it is no different in kingdom service. What we use to satiate our needs for love, security, significance, and purpose cannot sustain us in the continuing process of God's moving us from glory to glory.

Embracing the reality that the life you previously lived is not worth the battle to resist the life God has waiting will occur once you have faithfully moved through the process of obscurity.

ADAM'S BREAKOUT

That first cycle of obscurity did something completely amazing to me. Like the caterpillar that enters into the cocoon, not completely understanding the pain or awkwardness of the coming metamorphosis, I committed to the process. But once I was in the middle of the process, I wanted out! But it is within the fire that we are forged in a new purity and strength. I was not coming out of the heat anytime soon.

When I was thirteen years old, our family had an experience with the person of the Holy Spirit that transformed our lives. What we read in the Book of Acts began to be a part of our daily life in Christ. We became very accustomed to miracles and the gifts of the Spirit as listed in 1 Corinthians 12.

Prayer meetings, Bible studies, home groups, even engagements with the unchurched would have these moments where the Holy Spirit would touch us through prophecy, words of knowledge, words of wisdom, miracles, and so on. Almost every gathering I was a part of, someone would call out to me with a word of prophesy. The word from God was almost always the same: "God's hand is upon you. He is separating you out unto Himself. He is going to use you to touch the world. You will be a revivalist. You will have a special gift to reach the younger generation and your life will be marked by the supernatural."

These "messages" from God would come from people who did not know me, nor were they aware that others had spoken similar things over my life. I received those Prophecies as my "life's purpose," and I lived every day without anything else in mind. My security, my significance, and my confidence were completely wrapped in living God's purpose for my life. It was these Prophecies that guided me on where to live, what to study, whom to marry, who to surround myself with, and who not to surround myself with.

God kissed everything my wife and I put our hands to. In the mid-nineties, we had one of the largest youth ministries in the country. Fifty students a week were making first-time decisions for Christ. We had one hundred and twenty-five student-led small groups. We were one of only a handful of multiracial youth ministries in the country. Every Wednesday night was marked by miracles and transformation. The local judges deemed our student-led small groups as the best rehab option for troubled kids, so before sentencing offenders to "juvie" they would make them join a student-led small group. We had a 95 percent turnaround rate.

The success of fulfilling purpose was indescribable! Every day my wife and I would look at each other and say, "This is it! This is what life is all about."

And then in a flash, it was all gone. What happened, you ask? Well, like what often happens, leadership decided to shift and we were not included in that shift. Was my identity tied to the work we had been doing? Yes! Was my sense of security now stolen from me? Absolutely! Did I feel as though others were used by the enemy to shipwreck my purpose and destiny? You better believe I did!

Since this was my first time in the cocoon of obscurity, all I could see was the breaking down of what I had been. You see, when the caterpillar begins the metamorphosis, every bit of its identifiable parts turns to sludge—the tissue of the caterpillar completely breaks down, but its DNA does not. At some point the breakdown process is completed and the remaking process begins. I can honestly say I never imagined that something beautiful was being established within that first round of obscurity, but it was.

Unbeknownst to me, it was through that pain that my love was deepening for the Savior. Somehow, significance shifted away from what I was accomplishing to what I was becoming. Oh, and purpose stopped being a distant destination and became a daily expression. Yeah, I hated that first round of obscurity, but what emerged from the cocoon was much more beautiful than what went in.

SCOTT'S BREAKOUT

God's design for our life is so incredibly perfect that it's a crying shame we mess it up so badly, so often. But the truth is also that sometimes our destructive dysfunction was implanted like a time-delayed bomb that was activated in our childhood and finally detonated when we became adults.

In His original plan, God satisfied Adam's and Eve's every desire. They hung out with God in the cool of the day, had plenty to eat, lots of meaningful work to accomplish, and were both naked. Now, when I talk about being naked, yeah, they didn't wear clothes, but beyond the junior high snickering, nakedness also meant open, vulnerable, and totally transparent.

In that piece of heaven on earth within God's presence, mankind's needs for love, security, significance, and purpose were intended to be fulfilled by the Father. It was an act of selfish, sinful desire (eating from the forbidden Tree of the Knowledge of Good and Evil) to meet those needs on their own terms that created the separation from God's intimate presence. Yes, sin then, just like sin now, breaks our seamless bond with God. It was within sin's gap that the fulfillment of mankind's deepest needs became obscured.

No longer was the outpouring of love, security, significance, and purpose an internal refreshing by God. It continued to be a fruitless task to meet our own needs. Moving forward a few thousand years, I found myself seeking love, security, significance, and purpose as a child just as any human should. It is a need transcending our DNA because it was a core element of mankind's connection with God. It really is no different from being hungry for food, so we go looking for food. Even if it is junk food from the pantry or that carton of milk that may or may not be expired, our judgement becomes lax to say the least.

My childhood was dominated by an imposing father. He ruled over everyone in the family, including my mother. His weapon was physical intimidation and silence. We were not allowed to express any type of emotion, fear, or joy. Never once did he ever say anything affirming or nice. The idea of him saying "I love you" was laughable.

Of course, there was nothing funny about it. Even as I sat by his hospital bed in his last hours of life, I tried desperately to get him to say those three words. I would have been ecstatic with a "Good job" or a thumbs-up. After fifty years of longing to hear "I love you" with my dad's final breath, he took those words to the grave with him.

The dysfunctional dynamic with my father damaged our entire family. There are seven siblings—five boys and two girls. Of those, five of us are responsible for twelve divorces, eleven marriages, two kids out of wedlock, and an array of addictions, disorders, and disconnected relationships with our own children and each other as siblings.

Why?

None of us, and by us, I mean all seven siblings, had ever known the satisfaction of having our deepest needs met. God was never introduced to us as a family by our parents, so the concept of a heavenly God was frightening to a child who only knew fear and intimidation from his earthly father. We were completely dependent upon our parents for satisfying our needs from external means.

We grew up in a home without love shown or spoken. Violence and abuse robbed us of security in our home, our beds, or our own lives. We were bullied and abused beyond ever feeling significant to our parents, much less anyone outside the nuclear family unit. And other than being made to feel as if we were household hinderances, purpose was handed out as chores and busywork to keep us out of the way.

What I did not understand until I had come through my own season of obscurity was that the five of us who suffered in chaos and despair over the course of our lives were not unlucky. My other two siblings who have both been married to their spouses almost and over forty years didn't grow up in a bubble. They were in that same home environment, and carry scars from the bedlam, but they had one thing that made the difference—God.

Both siblings engaged in church once married and remained entrenched in a faith walk that has sustained their marriages, raising their families, and also becoming godly grandparents. Part of moving toward God for having their deepest needs met also meant a healthy separation from the toxic nature of harm that remained with the rest of us. I'm not saying they are perfect. They hurt for their past just as I do, but Christ gave them hope where I wallowed in helplessness. They drank from the living water that quenched their thirst while I lived in a state of being spiritually parched because of my dependence upon parents who did not have the living water to give me.

When you have a God-imparted thirst for love, security, significance, and purpose, there is nothing on this earth that can quench it. Not sex, drugs, alcohol, porn, money, title, or accolades—*nothing*. Everything I tried left me empty. I was chosen as a chief of police, and immediately I needed to administer a larger agency. I earned a master's degree, and I immediately pursued a PhD. But even that was not enough. I married the woman of my heart's desire, and I began to worry that there was someone else better for me. Nothing I ever accomplished would fill my deepest needs except the love of Jesus Christ.

My personal journey through obscurity showed me that important truth. My trials stripped me of everything I tried to clothe myself with and left me bare. It was only when God the awesome, loving Father placed a white robe across my shoulders did I understand the fullness of what my heart had always longed for. Only then was I overwhelmed with love, security, significance, and purpose. Thank God for getting me back to the garden.

6

THE CHOICE OF FEAR OR FAITH

THERE IS an old American Indian nugget of wisdom involving an elder explaining to his grandson the truth of life.

"A fight is going on inside me," he said to the boy.

"It is a terrible fight between two wolves. One is evil—he is anger, envy, sorrow, regret, greed, arrogance, self-pity, guilt, resentment, inferiority, lies, false pride, superiority, and ego."

The elder continued, "The other is good—he is joy, peace, love, hope, serenity, humility, kindness, benevolence, empathy, generosity, truth, compassion, and faith. The same fight is going on inside you—and inside every other person too."

Wide eyed, the grandson thought about it for a minute and then asked his grandfather: "Which wolf will win?"

The old man simply replied, "The one you feed."

CHOICE

The choice is yours. This is so important to accept, because while we have shared that obscurity is not a punishment but a gift in waiting, you should also understand God is not forcing you into this season.

Moses did not have to sit at the burning bush, David did not have to swing that sling, and Paul did not have to go to see Ananias.

In the prompting, there is a call to action which is or is not followed by obedience. God will not punish you, but He sure will not impart His gift within you. The dicey thing about choices is that even if you decide not to choose, it is still indeed a choice. It was a choice that ushered you into the season of obscurity to start with, so choose wisely.

Had you chosen not to respond to God's call or whatever it was you felt moved you into making a move that activated your season, the reality is, you would not have remained static in the current phase of life. Times change, and even if you had clung to a post within safe harbor, storms would still rage, waters would still rise, and winds would still howl. There is no neutral position, so it was either choose or have choice chosen for you.

Although the parable of the great banquet in Luke 14 addresses the invitation of the Gentiles into God's kingdom once the Jews rejected Him, it is also an important lesson in accepting or rejecting His invitation to growth seasons in the kingdom. The takeaway here is to choose wisely.

When one of those at the table with him heard this, he said to Jesus,

"Blessed is the one who will eat at the feast in the kingdom of God."

Jesus replied: "A certain man was preparing a great banquet and invited many guests. At the time of the banquet he sent his servant to tell those who had been invited, 'Come, for everything is now ready.'

"But they all alike began to make excuses.

The first said, 'I have just bought a field, and I must go and see it. Please excuse me.'

"Another said, 'I have just bought five yoke of oxen, and I'm on my way to try them out. Please excuse me.'

"Still another said, 'I just got married, so I can't come.'

"The servant came back and reported this to his master. Then the owner of the house became angry and ordered his servant, 'Go out quickly into the streets

and alleys of the town and bring in the poor, the crippled, the blind and the lame.'

"'Sir,' the servant said, 'what you ordered has been done, but there is still room.'

"Then the master told his servant, 'Go out to the roads and country lanes and compel them to come in, so that my house will be full. I tell you, not one of those who were invited will get a taste of my banquet.'"

— LUKE 14:15–24 (NIV)

We completely understand what you are experiencing. Had we both breezed through our respective seasons of obscurity, there would have been no urgency to write this book. Also, the initial bond connecting us through overcoming adversity would have been lost. Lastly, had we not entered into an atmosphere of feeding our good wolf, there would have been the prolonged consequence of faithless disobedience similar to that of God's people as they were poised to enter His Promised Land.

Make no mistake, if you choose to remain in obscurity, you will eventually die in your wilderness. Pretending to leave the old baggage of the life you were called out of will not produce the fruits necessary to sustain your journey into the Promised Land.

He brought us out from there in order to bring us in, to give us the land which He had sworn to our fathers.

— DEUTERONOMY 6:23 (KJV)

Of course, that prompts us to ask a favorite question: are you a grasshopper or giant killer?

And there we saw the Nephilim (the sons of Anak, who come from the Nephilim), and we seemed to ourselves like grasshoppers, and so we seemed to them.

— NUMBERS 13:33 (ESV)

GRASSHOPPER OR GIANT KILLER

In much the same way God called you out, He also makes a promise to protect and provide for you. He adores you. An example long preceding anything you have ever experienced is the exodus of God's children from the grips of cruel Egyptian oppression. Their calling was an opportunity for mass transformation from slavery into a free people blessed beyond imagination in their Promised Land.

They experienced doubt in the veracity of God's calling. Although there was an iron-clad assurance of a better life in an environment created by God himself, the Israelites stumbled in their obedience and faith walk. While they were in the midst of obscurity, they often pined for the days of old. Yes, those very same days of misery and death at the hands of vicious taskmasters.

Does that seem familiar—when we find ourselves off-center of where we think we should be? We have that tendency to romanticize the good old days, no matter if they were good or just old.

Despite God's gift of an iron-clad promise (Jeremiah 29:11), once we have moved our needle the slightest bit past what we were once used to, our discomfort level hits red zone alert status. It is a natural inclination to resist change in the unknown zone. Even good stress (eustress) is stressful and compounding the mystery with the loss of what once was is understandable. But that is also an indication of self-reliance. Let's commit to taking our shoes off on the holy ground of this God-encountered obscurity because this choice determines whether you are a grasshopper or giant killer.

Prior to the Israelites claiming the Promised Land, God instructed Moses to send spies into the region. The group of twelve men representing each of the tribes of Israel were assigned to infiltrate Canaan for forty days before reporting back whether it was ready to be conquered.

Armed with the assurance of God, the twelve entered into, observed, and returned to report their findings to Moses. Ten of the spies gave negative reports. Although the land was the way God described it as flowing with milk and honey, they feared the inhabitants. Actually, the people they saw were trespassing upon God's land, yet ten of them agreed that the occupants were too mighty to defeat, and fear commanded their decision-making process.

Fear requires a choice to allow yourself to be directed by strong and unpleasant emotions. Faith, on the other hand, requires that you choose to press into and live within it, without being attached to the unsteady swing of emotion. Unlike the stifling feelings of fear, faith is the liberating conviction in what is not seen, yet not demanding evidence. It is much easier to choose fear, but you surrender the promise of a life in the faith of God's blessings.

Now faith is the substance of things hoped for, the evidence of things not seen.

— *HEBREWS 11:1 (KJV)*

Isn't it amazing what fear, even in contrast to the facts presented, can make us do? The ten spies who saw the promised condition of a bountiful land were blinded by fear. They decided to slant the facts in a way to discourage Moses and the nation of Israel from claiming their ordained Promised Land. They not only reported on what they observed about the bountiful lands and how they felt personally about how invincible the inhabitants were, but the ten spies were so driven by fear that they made assumptions about what the inhabitants thought about them: "*and we seemed to ourselves like grasshoppers, and so we seemed to them.*"

How often has fear gripped you in the course of your wilderness season? Have you arrived at the cusp of exiting the darkness, yet lingering fear of the unknown influenced you to slant the reality of where you are in the movement toward change? We are in a place where we can begin to discuss exiting obscurity, but your response in these closing moments has increasingly important consequences.

The fear choice that drove ten spies to deal falsely with facts and ignited a national revolt against the promise of God brought severe consequences against them. Every single adult citizen of Israel lost out on the gift of an unbelievably blessed life in their Promised Land. They wandered around the wilderness until all of them died in their darkness instead of living with joy in the light of transformational change.

Everyone, that is, except Caleb and Joshua of course. They understood the potential of entering God's Promised Land; they were faithful about exiting obscurity; and they never hesitated to overcome whatever or whoever stood in the way of receiving God's gifts of anointing.

Because this is so applicable to what you are walking through, take a moment to read what Joshua said in an effort to change the minds of the fearful. Sometimes these are conversations we must have with ourselves. We have underlined sections for emphasis.

> *The land we passed through and explored is exceedingly good. If the Lord is pleased with us, he will lead us into that land, a land flowing with milk and honey, and will give it to us. Only do not rebel against the Lord. And do not be afraid of the people of the land, because we will devour them. Their protection is gone, but the Lord is with us. Do not be afraid of them.*

> — *NUMBERS 14:7–9*

When you find yourself in unexpected circumstances, it is not uncommon to pine for the old days. They may have been terrible, but at least you knew the rules of the game. We also understand that obscurity brings our fears to the surface because it is only within these seasons that we are no longer tethered to the safety straps of what it was we once knew. There can be an unsettling silence in the storm when you cry out and God does not sweep in and rescue you—again.

This is not the season to decide out of fear that it is better to jump out of the boat as opposed to sticking with it. Cling to the faith that you are not alone in the storm, nor are you alone in the boat. Looking at Mark 4:35–41 is an excellent illustration of where you are and who is with you.

Sometimes when we look at life from a different perspective, we see new truths revealed in the most obscure of times. If fear has crept up your spine like the cold slither of a serpent's slide, then take heed of this verse. It is so beautiful and liberating. Just when we begin to fret over being abandoned and left in our season of obscurity, we see in Mark 4 that Jesus says to the disciples, "Let us go over to the other side."

You know what this means to you? It means you will pass through to the other side. That alone should be assurance in rejoicing over your struggles coming to an end. Notice Jesus did not say, "I hope we make it" or, "With any luck we might get there." No, He declaratively said with full assurance that they were going over to the other side. Jesus didn't have to check the Weather Channel or His water conditions app. He knew that no matter the storms in life, He, they, and you were going over to the other side.

Still unsure about your choice? How about what Mark says next, "Leaving the crowd behind, they took him along." That was their best decision yet—they took Jesus with them. Guess what? You should too. You will leave your crowd behind during this season. It may be physical separation or an emotional parting for a season, but obscurity also involves isolation (think of Jesus being tempted in His wilderness for forty days—Matthew 4:1–11). Once you step out into the opportunity for gaining God's new anointing, remember it's not a solo act. Jesus was and continues to be close by your side.

Often neglected because of the depth of this verse is the truth that although you are isolated either physically or perceptually, there are others around you who are managing their way through similar seasons: "There were also other boats with him." (Mark 4:36)

That day we first met after church to share our respective testimonies was no coincidence. Divine alignment made sure both of our boats were in the same waters so that we understood neither was alone and that upon those trials of growth and change, others were paddling there as well.

The difference between our natural perception and spiritual reality is stark by comparison. Listening to others share their wilderness experiences, and based upon where they are along the journey, allows for sweeping ranges in variances of testimonies. But once the certainty of their experience is actualized, it leans closer to spiritual fact. Mark's description of the storm tells of a furious uprising that almost caused them to sink. Despite this, not only was Jesus in the boat and not panicking, He was asleep on a cushion: "A furious squall came up, and the waves broke over the boat, so that it was nearly swamped. Jesus was in the stern, sleeping on a cushion." (Mark 4:37–38) Doesn't that give you a cozy reassurance that we are not alone in this?

Let's jump past the disciples' reactions and see exactly what Jesus did in the midst of their deepest doubts. "'Quiet! Be still!' Then the wind died down and it was completely calm." (Mark 4:39) He calmed the storm. He did not just calm it, but it was completely calm. Also, don't miss the point that when He commanded, "Quiet! Be still!" that it was meant for the disciples as well. If you have been in the struggle, your faith is fading into fear and you are tempted to make a run (or swim) for it, heed the words of the one who has invited you to go over to the other side. "Quiet! Be still!"

Did you ever just want to shake some sense into the disciples? Seriously, they were right there with Jesus Christ himself, in the flesh. He couldn't have been more real than in the years they spent together, and still they chose fear over faith. We are not judging them because we have been there too. That is why they have endured and connect to our hearts over the centuries.

What we want you to know without a doubt is that the crisis you may be experiencing in your storm does not mean Jesus needs to wake up and rescue you from the turmoil. He is there and has already promised you safe passage to the other side, but it is the turmoil that Jesus knows will soon become your testimony. It is the gift from God to lead you closer into your walk with Christ. If you want deeper waters to withstand life's storms, you first must go through the storms of deep waters.

Jesus has not abandoned the boat. He is right there with you, and His response of sleeping on a cushion was not as much about needing a nap as it is an example for you to model in the midst of obscurity's storms. Whether you cross water or a bridge, you are almost to the other side, so choose to stay in the boat, choose to stick close to Christ, and choose to wait on Him to act.

Happy sailing!

> That day when evening came, he said to his disciples, "Let us go over to the other side." Leaving the crowd behind, they took him along, just as he was, in the boat. There were also other boats with him. A furious squall came up, and the waves broke over the boat, so that it was nearly swamped. Jesus was in the stern, sleeping on a cushion. The disciples woke him and said to him, "Teacher, don't you

care if we drown?" He got up, rebuked the wind and said to the waves, "Quiet! Be
still!" Then the wind died down and it was completely calm. He said to his
disciples, "Why are you so afraid? Do you still have no faith?" They were terrified
and asked each other, "Who is this? Even the wind and the waves obey him!"

— MARK 4:35–41

ADAM'S BREAKOUT

A very successful pastor friend of mine once said, "I never knew inse-
curity until I started planting a church." Truer words have never been
spoken. We were just a couple years into church planting when I'd had
enough. I'd followed the Lord into this venture, and it simply was not
working.

We had a small team that was quickly losing their confidence as to the
success of our endeavor. We had minuscule resources, but our greatest
hindrance was we had no building to call home. No place to point to as
ours. Nowhere to hang a sign, or even an address to put on a website.
Every day for eighteen months I went about trying to secure a place to
call ours.

I met with sellers to no avail. The independent school district in our
area would have nothing to do with us. I met with pastors hoping to
share space, but NOTHING. In those eighteen months, I walked
through thirty-two potential locations, had ten offers rejected, two
contracts absolved, multiple realtors laugh in our face, and every bank
we approached deny us lending. I was done!

I was already preparing an exit strategy when I met Coach Mike. I had
been invited to play in a local charity golf tournament. Our team of
four had a dropout so at the last minute, Coach Mike was invited to
play with us. Mike had spent many years as an executive pastor in a
megachurch in Seattle. His wisdom and leadership led many
successful business leaders to seek out his guidance.

This propelled him into life coaching. After years of coaching Fortune
500 CEOs on the West Coast, God reassigned him to McKinney, Texas.
Yep, Mike was starting over as a church planter in his fifties. We had
barely teed off the first hole when Mike turned to me and asked,

"How's the church plant going?" He graciously listened to me whine and complain the entire front nine.

Every suggestion he made I came back with ten reasons it could not work in my situation. By the time we were rounding the eighteenth hole he had whittled through all of my excuses. His confidence was contagious! He had me dreaming again. I had not realized the impact those eighteen months of attempting to secure a facility had on my faith. I was literally out of faith.

Coach Mike's willingness to start over again was the nudge I needed to choose faith instead of fear. In that moment, I needed someone of experience to patiently wade with me through my fears and disappointments. I needed someone to help me pick up all the failed attempts, evaluate them properly, and develop a strategy worth trying again. I needed to draw from someone else's courage because my faith account was overdrawn. I needed a Coach Mike, and in my darkest moment, God sent him to me free of charge.

Within three months of first meeting Coach Mike, we were given a building five times beyond anything I could have hoped for. Our church exploded and the rest is, as they say, history. Go find your Coach Mike. He may just have that nudge of faith you need. Who knows, maybe you will get to experience a life-changing miracle too.

SCOTT'S BREAKOUT

Sitting across from the Christian counselor, I pressed my tattooed arms across my chest and sunk back into the chair. I had made sure to wear my gnarliest Harley-Davidson T-shirt and scuffed leather motorcycle boots. I had selected the one chair in his office that allowed me to sit higher than him, because I understood the dynamics of interrogations and high-stakes negotiations. It was my marriage on the line, and to an even bigger extent, my very life. Yeah, I was in it to win it, but I had defined victory on that first visit as intimidating and manipulating that young counselor into seeing everything my way.

I recall the warm feeling of self-satisfaction as he admitted that I was intimidating and had a dynamic personality. I had played my cards just as I planned. It was a tactical combination of physical appearance and feeding him with a steady stream of my background in police special operations, undercover work, and SWAT. Oh, and I was sure to drop a few academic boasts about holding a PhD as well. It was just a matter of time until he'd pat me on the back, call my wife into the office, and explain to her that I was right and she was overreacting.

Just before I let out a chuckle and thanked him for being so attentive, he rubbed his chin with his finger and thumb. He said, "Scott, you've got an unteachable spirit." I leaned back and recrossed my arms to signal that I was not pleased with what he'd just said. Then he said with more sternness in his voice than I thought him capable of, "And there's nothing I can or will do for you. You're wasting my time and yours, so you and your wife can leave."

Wow! I didn't see that one coming.

I had a choice to make. Submitting to counseling was a nonnegotiable item where my marriage was concerned. Leah had suffered through adultery, my law enforcement career, my terrible transition into retirement, the darkest of obscurity as past pain, PTSD, and suicide ideation became more than I could hide without the façade of the badge. There was no way we could go on living like that. I knew what choice I had to make, and it had nothing to do with intimidation, interrogations, or manipulation. It was time to surrender.

It was tough going back the next week, but I'd prayed about it and God set a peace upon me. No longer was I doing this to check off a box for Leah, but I understood that there were giants in my life that had resided in my Promised Land for decades. While I had always considered myself tough and unafraid, the truth was, I was no better than one of those ten spies who manufactured their own truth to avoid the confrontations required for freedom. I'll admit it—I was a grasshopper.

The core-level transformation that occurred over that week was like nothing I had ever experienced. I had been in my wilderness season and knew that my past could no longer bear control on life that was yet to become. One of the choices I made was that I had no ability to control that scenario. Honestly, it was weird and uncomfortable. There had been very little, during most of my adult life, that I hadn't been able to control. And in hindsight, when I wasn't able to manipulate it, I would usually opt for destroying it.

Choosing to surrender to the truth was not easy. But understanding it was only by the grace of Jesus Christ that I had come that far, I was willing to hand over the rest of the journey to Him. Heading back to see that counselor, I knew I owed him an apology. I also knew that the hard exterior of old jeans and biker T-shirts was not representative of what was going on with my interior. I decided to dress more in line with who God was calling me to be and not the manipulator I always thought I had to present to others. Not that clothes made me who I was or wasn't, but I chose to make the difference inside and out.

I think he expected the shift and was gracious in accepting my apology. Over the course of that next year, Leah and I experienced unimaginable changes in our own lives and our marriage. Possibly the most amazing affirmation of God's hand at work through my season of transitioning was moving from a grasshopper to a giant killer. What giants are you ready to slay?

7

CROSSING THE BRIDGE OF OBSCURITY

THERE ARE key decision-making opportunities in life, which we either approach voluntarily or have them thrust upon us. While seasons of obscurity may launch with obedience to God's calling, the experience once within the cycle becomes unexpected and often filled with struggle. This is where the illustration of bridge-crossing becomes the perfect example for helping you move with enthusiasm along what has been described as God's crucible.

Not everyone will choose to cross the bridge of obscurity. That is perfectly well with God, and hopefully well with your soul. God does not force His will upon us. Obscurity is not punishment; it is a gift-giving process. Part of that process requires faithful action on your part. That action involves crossings that once completed can never return you to the person you were prior to that action. Our prayer is that you will activate your anointing through making the choice to cross that bridge.

Every believer will be presented with an opportunity to cross the bridge of obscurity. Obscurity is defined as the state of being unknown, inconspicuous, unimportant, difficult to understand, lack of adequate illumination, not famous, or hidden. At some point in our lives all of us will have a season, or even many seasons, that can be described by one or more of the previous words.

Perhaps you are crossing this bridge as we speak, or maybe you have already crossed it. Either way, the words in this chapter will ring true. And for those of you that have not yet experienced obscurity, if you are called by God, you will—trust us. You see, obscurity is the tool God uses to develop character in our lives that cannot be developed any other way. He uses the dark, hidden places to show us that who we are in Christ is not determined by our activity, our position, our title, or the perception others have of us.

Christian culture is filled with admonitions such as "you'll do great things in the kingdom" or "be somebody" or "make a difference" or "change the world." While these are all encouraging phrases, they can lead people to believe that they are unimportant if they are not "making their mark."

The desire for greatness is within us, but the world has an upside-down ideology regarding fame and fortune. Remember, Christ taught us that the greatest in the kingdom would be a servant. Matthew 20:26–28 says, "Whoever wants to become great among you must be your servant, and whoever wants to be first must be your slave—just as the Son of Man did not come to be served, but to serve, and to give his life as a ransom for many." Christ spent thirty years in obscurity to be prepared for three years of ministry!

The seasons of obscurity can be the hardest seasons in our lives. Until we "arrive" at the place where we feel we are doing something important, it is easy to be continually dissatisfied in other roles. We tend to resent the waiting. But the times of obscurity are designed to bring us into maturity, to tenderize our hearts with the kind of humility required to experience success and not fall prey to pride.

Too many gifted individuals have lost their place of influence because their charisma took them higher than their character could keep them. Charismatic people are attractive, and we are drawn to their effervescence, their gifts, their talents, and even their anointing. But God is not glorified through fallen ministries and believers who succumb to worldly lifestyles. God is glorified by those whose character is even stronger than their charisma, those who will not bow a knee to temptation, those who have lived quietly and unknown, embraced the hiddenness, and crossed the bridge of obscurity with integrity and unshakeable faith.

If we do not embrace the season of obscurity, we will not be prepared for our season of influence. God wants us all to have that moment when we think—*This is it. This is what I was created for*—but that time will only come through preparation and faithfulness. It is imperative that when you reach that moment, you are the person you are supposed to be at that time.

Some of you can look back and see your times of obscurity; you can read your journal entries, and even remember your lamentations. Some of you are reading this with tears in your eyes, the pang of loneliness still fresh. You know you are in a hidden place now and it's tough. Others still are not sure about this bridge and are not even sure if they can cross it. Review the list below to determine where you might be in your journey:

You Need to Cross the Bridge of Obscurity if:

- It's really hard when someone else gets credit for something you did.
- You feel less of a person if you are not accomplishing something others consider significant.
- You feel like you need to embellish or exaggerate your life.
- Seeing your name in print or in lights excites you.
- Having people answer to you makes you feel important. (Leadership is God-made, but we must be careful not to enjoy bossing people around or feeling superior.)
- You are jealous when you see someone else doing what God has called you to do. (You might even think, *I could do that so much better!*)
- It hurts when people ask what you do or where you live.

It is interesting when we look back on our own times of obscurity. Often, we were following the plan of God for our lives, but to others we were crazy. Sometimes, others' opinions or disapproval can make us question the voice of God in our lives. Many times, His plan for us is the polar opposite of His plan for those closest to us. Obscurity teaches us to hear His voice more clearly and rely on His faithfulness.

We learn to seek His approval, rather than man's. In the lonely, hidden times, we become God-focused, rather than man-focused. When we have crossed the bridge of obscurity, it is easy to see how He used it to mold our character, but in the midst of the bridge, disappointment and uncertainty arise.

Important Points Regarding Obscurity

Crossing the bridge of obscurity is inevitable, so let's prepare ourselves to understand its value and importance in our lives.

- **Key elements of your character can only be formed through obscurity**

Joseph's character was developed through the pit, the temptations, and imprisonment. Though we would love to think that we could jump from being the favorite son right into the palace, most of us need the time and pressure that produces patience and perfection in our lives.

James 1:2–4 tells us, "Consider it pure joy, my brothers and sisters, whenever you face trials of many kinds, because you know that the testing of your faith produces perseverance. Let perseverance finish its work so that you may be mature and complete, not lacking anything." Though most of us like the idea of maturity and completeness, the process is always, always difficult!

The trial of obscurity teaches us dependence on God; it increases our faith and develops integrity; we learn contentment, endurance, patience, and humility. Best of all, if we cross the bridge of obscurity successfully, we will have gained a servant's heart. Your time in the cave helps you develop a deeper trust in God. It gives you fresh perspective on your commitment to Him. If we never encounter diffi-culty, we will never know the depth (or lack thereof) of our commit-ment to Christ.

Diamonds and graphite are made from the same original substance—carbon—the only difference in what they become is their external expe-rience. Graphite is one of the softest elements in the world and diamonds are one of the hardest elements in the world. Diamonds are formed from intense heat in the deep dark places in the earth. The pressure, heat, and obscurity turn the carbon into a diamond. Diamonds are valuable and priceless, and they were formed in intense conditions. Remember, you also are being transformed into the likeness of Christ—from common, to priceless!

- **Obscurity may come when you least expect it**

Moses grew up a prince in a palace. He then spent years in the desert as a shepherd, as well as the last of his life in the desert, never to see the Promised Land. David began as a shepherd, became a giant killer and great warrior, and was hailed as the next king, only to end up running from Saul for many years, spending some of that time in the cave of Adullam.

- **Pride and success worsen the sting of obscurity**

David was fine as a shepherd, but once he killed Goliath and received some notoriety, he felt let down and discouraged that Saul wanted to kill him. 1 Samuel 27:1 says, "Then David said in his heart, 'Now I shall perish one day by the hand of Saul. There is nothing better for me than that I should escape to the land of the Philistines. Then Saul will despair of seeking me any longer within the borders of Israel, and I shall escape out of his hand.'" Success was almost in his grasp, so the disappointment was more severe. When you are greatly gifted or see success within your reach, obscurity can be even more challenging.

- **Pursuing contentment is the only way to cross the bridge of obscurity**

Paul gave us a great example of contentment in Philippians 4:12; he said, "I know what it is to be in need, and I know what it is to have plenty. I have learned the secret of being content in any and every situation, whether well fed or hungry, whether living in plenty or in want."

We have become an instant gratification society. God is not on microwave time. His timing is perfect, and He is determined to teach us patience. The season does not have to define you—you can define the season through contentment. Enjoy the simplicity. The Roman poet Ovid once said, "Well has he lived who has lived well in obscurity."

- **The glory of victory will find you**

You do not have to seek out significance. Jennie Riddle, the composer of "Revelation Song," wrote it while being a homemaker and after putting her baby down for a nap. It has been said that part of the song was composed in her laundry room! God decides the right moment and the right vehicle; it is our job to be ready when our moment comes. The successes will find you. You don't have to pursue people of influence to become influential. If you will flourish in obscurity, God will reveal you in His time.

Consider Jael, a woman now known in Israel's history as a hero. The Israelites had been oppressed by Sisera, the commander of the Canaanite army, for two decades; they cried to the Lord for help. The Lord responded and promised that Sisera would be defeated. Jael was in her tent, going about her daily housewife chores just like she would any other day (often housewives live lives of obscurity). Sisera fled from the site of the battle and sought refuge in her tent. Judges 4:18–21 says,

> Jael went out to meet Sisera and said to him, "Come, my lord, come right in. Don't be afraid." So he entered her tent, and she covered him with a blanket. "I'm thirsty," he said. "Please give me some water." She opened a skin of milk, gave him a drink, and covered him up. "Stand in the doorway of the tent," he told her. "If someone comes by and asks you, 'Is anyone in there?' say 'No.'" But Jael, Heber's wife, picked up a tent peg and a hammer and went quietly to him while he lay fast asleep, exhausted. She drove the peg through his temple into the ground, and he died.

So suddenly, Jael, a woman likely living in obscurity, is an Israelite hero! Do you ever wonder how she had the courage or even the physical strength to do what she did? Could it be that her muscles, both spiritual and physical, had been developing during the years of obscurity? Have you considered that your hidden place may also become your place of victory?

Perhaps like Sisera, the enemy in your life has become unaware of the power you possess, the power that has been growing in you in the dark seasons! While the enemy sleeps, God is placing the power to destroy him in your hands. Think about it! While loneliness can seem unbearable and lack of recognition grows old, Christ can use this secret time to build you into an ominous threat to the kingdom of darkness!

Take solace in knowing that the victories God intends for your life will find you. Jael knew that it was not where she was that made her significant, but rather WHO she was. When her moment came, she had the fortitude to do what needed to be done. Rather than resist our time of obscurity, we must embrace it, knowing that we are being made ready for our moment in time.

God promises us that our personal breakthrough will come as we minister to the needs of others. Isaiah 58:10 says, "And if you spend yourselves in behalf of the hungry and satisfy the needs of the oppressed, then your light will rise in the darkness, and your night will become like the noonday."

He doesn't tell us to seek out influential people, but rather minister to the least of these. God always rewards servanthood. Proverbs 22:29 tells us "Do you see someone skilled in their work? They will serve before kings; they will not serve before officials of low rank." Then, in Proverbs 18:16 we are reminded that, "A man's gift makes room for him and brings him before great men" (NKJV). In other words, dear reader, be faithful to Him and His Word, and your time will come!

Although we all dread a season (or lifetime) of obscurity, it is absolutely necessary to our development as trusted leaders. It is only in the "unknown" times that key components of our character can be forged strong so that we are able to bear the weight of future successes. Though it is not easy, embrace the bridge of obscurity when it comes.

Move forward, step-by-step, trusting God's timing and His methods. Do not try to manipulate the time frame, but rather find contentment knowing that the diamond is formed in the darkness. The gifts and talents He has given you are first for Him—sing when no one hears you sing; preach when no one hears you preach; write when no one reads your words. Ephesians 6:7 reminds us to "Serve wholeheartedly, as if you were serving the Lord, not people."

Embrace the bridge of obscurity and get to know your God. Intimacy with Him is formed in the lonely times, for in the quiet we can best hear His whisper.

ADAM'S BREAKOUT

After thirty years of caring for and loving on leaders, God revealed to me insights on just how to navigate through obscurity. I had once expected these revelations to hold deep, mysterious truths that few knew the honor to attain. I was ready to receive God's wisdom and a little anxious at the potential for absorbing such wisdom. In God's infinite glory, I was taught to punt.

That's right. The main lesson I learned from God in how to help others navigate the matrix of their seasons in the wilderness was to drop back and punt. In football, there is nothing more discouraging for an offense that has worked so hard grinding it out on the field of battle than to find themselves in a helpless fourth and ten situation. There is no chance of scoring and moving the ball another ten yards. They might as well be moving it across the globe.

So what else was there to do but exactly what God showed me—punt.

When the plays that previously worked are not moving the ball, the enemy seems to know your every move, and teammates are not carrying their share of the burden—just punt.

But that sounds like giving up, right? It could be taken that way if your spirit is resistant to actually moving forward. In reality, it is letting go, and there is a big difference between the two. It is only after you have let go of all self-focused dreams of scoring on that one drive can you redirect and regroup to win the game.

Now is the perfect time to:

- stop complaining about what went wrong,
- stop replaying missed opportunities,
- stop glaring at others on your team who failed or hurt you, and
- stop identifying with how great your stats were coming into this game.

The best NFL quarterbacks are said to have the shortest memory span on the field. They throw an interception and forget about it. They miss a handoff and by the time they walk back to the huddle, it's forgotten.

Yes, even that seventy-yard touchdown pass they just threw to take the lead is forgotten before they reach the sidelines. Why? Because what is behind them is behind them. Their focus is on what is next, and yours should be too.

The apostle Paul said it like this:

> But one thing I do: Forgetting what is behind and straining toward what is ahead, I press on toward the goal.
>
> — *PHILIPPIANS 3:13–14 (NIV)*

Most people think the apostle Paul is saying to "forget" your failures, but he's not. He is telling us to forget about our successes, our trophies, and our heroic stats. Maybe it is better explained this way. Stop clinging to your job title, your golf score, and your latest portfolio uptick.

The apostle Paul was a prodigy. He was highly intelligent, extremely ambitious, and he was of proper pedigree, or as he put it:

> If anyone else thinks he has reasons to put confidence in the flesh, I have more: circumcised on the eighth day, of the people of Israel, of the tribe of Benjamin, a Hebrew of Hebrews; in regard to the law, a Pharisee; as for zeal, persecuting the church; as for legalistic righteousness, faultless.
>
> — *PHILIPPIANS 3:4–6 (NIV)*

See, when the apostle Paul turned to Christ, all of his success in Judaism was over. The years of hard work went down the drain. The respect due him was replaced with contempt. Those who had looked to him for leadership ostracized him and declared him the enemy. In our modern-day comparisons, his name plate was ripped off of the fancy office door, his country club membership was revoked, and he went bankrupt. Yet never in his life of earthly accolades had he ever gained so much more as when he lost it all.

When he says, "forgetting what is behind", he is not talking about short-term memory loss. The apostle Paul is encouraging us to stop resting on the laurels of past successes based on who we were, and instead, begin again new in Christ. Allow the spirit man inside of you to lay a new foundation so that your life's renovated structure of glory begins from an unshakable position of starting over at a bedrock ground floor.

Additionally, the apostle Paul encourages us with his second critical point to simply "press on to what is ahead." Easy, right? Dear friend, let it go so you can see what lies ahead and then start the process of "pressing."

Can you remember back before you tumbled into your wilderness season? Most of us do because we are still clinging on to what once used to be. But as we progress along the journey, the old, natural-centered person's recollection of what used to be important becomes a little foggy. I assure you that in those days before the chaos of obscurity there was a tenacity for getting what you thought was owed you.

Prior to the humility gained through our transformative season, we refused to take no for an answer. Even if it was detrimental to our own cause, we were going to get what was "ours." Remember that person?

Well, that fire is still within you except that instead of insistence and resistance, it burns for restoration and renewal. It's time to awaken out of your passivity and put that fervor to work. Start with what is in front of you no matter how lowly or worthless it may seem, press forward. What looks like failure in having to punt on a fourth down will actually lead to the victory at the end of the game.

SCOTT'S BREAKOUT

At some point in my life I thought it would be a great idea to pursue a PhD. I had previously given up the notion of being an educator back during my undergraduate studies and became a cop instead. Some people say it is basically the same profession except that I got to deal with the troubled kids later rather than during their childhoods. So, despite the negative casting, returning to the idea of teaching prompted my leap into a doctoral program.

I have always been interested in the way people within a society develop patterns and practices of life within smaller groupings called cultures. These micropockets of the larger society are distinctive, yet not regionally specific. Questions such as how earlier populations from seemingly disparate places on the globe developed similar languages, buildings from structures, temples to mounds, formed tribes and families, and even understood higher powers.

My doctoral dissertation was framed around my favorite anthropologist, Victor Turner. Yes, there are favorites in the field of anthropology! His work explained what he titled liminal transitions in life. They were threshold experiences that, once moved through, the person could never go back to who they once were. For example, accepting Jesus Christ as your Savior is the most transformational experience one can enjoy. Although that person will sin, and may even backslide, they can never return to the state of being prior to receiving salvation.

While the theory of liminality is a secular concept borne out of academic ideology, the concept of bridge-crossings is grounded in scriptural reference. The illustration of a series of crossings helps clarify the process of moving through seasons of obscurity. Like any bridge we face in life, there is a choice to move forward in God's blessings or take a seat as life and opportunity pass us by.

I want to share five important points regarding obscurity in my life in hopes that you may have gone through similar experiences. The first one that forms key elements of our character occurred in my life as I was removed from the spotlight of self-importance and into an isolation of surrender. It's easy to do the right thing when everyone is watching, and it's even easier to do the right thing when it's you who gets to define what the right thing is.

My profession provided the atmosphere where my character was defined by the job I did, not the God I served. Obviously, it was not an environment where change could or would occur. Moving into obscurity was most painful when I understood that God wanted me to serve His kingdom, but at fifty years old, I had no idea who I was. Once the title of police chief was retired, I was left with an empty husk. Yet, it was because of obscurity that I began to know exactly who I was. God gave me my new identity, but it was through the wilderness trials after crossing the bridge of obscurity that I accepted it and activated the new anointing.

The second point we offered was that obscurity may come when you least expect it. As I've shared before, I was in full stride in my career. A new four-year contract as chief of police that would have landed me at the steps of a full thirty-year pension, teaching college classes at night, and traveling the country as a national subject matter expert. Who would have ever imagined in a million years that months into my second term as chief I would walk into the mayor's office and retire? God did of course, and I am so thankful that He did. I can honestly say that knowing what I know now, I do not think I would be alive today had He not walked me through the wilderness of obscurity.

My life prior to having the chains of my past shattered was an egotistical exercise based on pride and self-success. I was my own idol, and despite the faith I had in Christ, when the chips were on the table, I was betting on me and my ability to manipulate every situation life threw at me. It was that same pride that stung every time I went out in public after retirement and no one knew or cared who I was or what I did. Honestly, I felt the world owed me just for being me. I did dangerous work and the new reality of no one acknowledging me for it was hurtful to my prideful ego. It was not until obscurity's lessons revealed the beauty and grace of having much less of me and so much more of Him. Reflecting Christ in my life was much more fulfilling than promoting me.

After crossing the bridge of obscurity, I entered into an atmosphere so supernatural that most of the time I was overwhelmed by God's presence. Although in the beginning of my journey I was unsure of what was happening in life, contentment served as an anchor in even the darkest of storms. Approaching the bridge of obscurity with fear, resistance, and a desperate grasp on your past will only prolong the periods of discomfort. Surrendering the journey to the one who charted your path brings contentment in the transformational changes like you have never known.

The final element in our five important points regarding obscurity is that the glory of victory will find you. How, you might ask? Remember, this is one of the most spiritual conversions you will ever experience. God started this work to bless you and He will make ways for you to apply the new gifts that He has imparted within you. As I began to see a light through my darkness, I tried to self-activate my new anointing. It was like a spectator running from out of the stands to call a play on the huddle. I found myself in situations that, although my heart was in the right place, I had no business being in.

Eventually, God opened the first door into ministry. It was inside a dilapidated building where men struggling with substance abuse and addictions would gather every Tuesday night. There was no stage, microphone, paved parking, or heat in the middle of winter. It was not where I had ever imagined finding glory. But as you probably already know, it was there that God activated my anointing and set my spiritual gifting of testimony for His glory ablaze. Yep, God's glory of victory will find you no matter where you are.

8

THRIVING IN OBSCURITY

THINK about the darkest days during your season of obscurity. We both thought we had outdone each other when we began sharing our testimonies. Having endured loss of influence, title, and pay all ranked up there, right? It's funny how perspective helps place truth back as priority. We have a mutual friend who you might have heard of, or if lucky enough, you've heard him speak. His name is Gene McGuire. Look him up. You will thank us.

As a seventeen-year-old boy, Gene was arrested for first-degree murder for a crime he didn't commit. Over the next thirty-five years, he paced a tiny prison cell. And after more than three decades in confinement, Gene was released when it was discovered he was wrongfully convicted and sentenced. Talk about a season of obscurity! Just like our heroes of old and their imprisonments, Gene did not waste those years being bitter. He came to know Jesus, and while still in prison, he was set free in Christ.

Even after heeding God's calling, Gene remained in obscurity behind prison walls for decades. Yet he began to thrive in the direst of modern environments. When he was freed from his life in prison, he continued the works God first placed in his heart so many years earlier. Thriving in Gene's obscurity meant maintaining a meaningful life behind bars by sharing God's Word and remaining a living example of Christ to other inmates and prison employees.

It still amazes us to consider thirty-five years in prison while wrongfully convicted, and even more incredible is his forgiving, servant's heart. With Gene's friendship and testimony as part of our reality, things like loss of influence or earning potential make our own stories dim in comparison.

Unfortunately, each of us experiencing seasons of obscurity find no solace in comparing the trials of each other to what means the most to us. This is not a case of comparison, but taking an opportunity to talk about thriving in those wilderness seasons. When approached in positivity, you will soon embrace that obscurity was not punishment.

Every occasion we get to speak with someone sharing their testimony about how dark and unexpectedly impossible life is, we focus on the reality that they are in the process of gift-getting. The irony is that there are opportunities for transformational change like no other time in your life. Is it challenging? Sure it is, but you have a choice on how to approach it, and only you can make that decision.

Let's talk about what thriving in obscurity looks like. Well, to be honest, it depends. Isn't that always the most horrible reply? But the truth is, no one enters into obscurity, processes through it, or exits in the same way. It depends on you. We have identified some common factors to help you maintain the proper posture as you proceed toward the inevitable.

It is not surprising to hear people share that they feel alone or abandoned, but in order for God to do His work in your life requires the potter to go directly hands on with the clay. Even though you don't notice His presence, God is fully present in your life.

Thriving in your walk begins with acknowledging that God is in charge. Next, it requires surrendering who you once perceived yourself to be. Willingness to walk in God's will as understood through prayer, Bible reading, meditation on His Word, and waiting on Him to move in your life is vital. Also knowing that in order for God to do a mighty work in your life requires that He work mightily in your life. That means you are not alone and have never been abandoned. God has never been so close to you as He is in this remodeling project!

ATTITUDE

The first and most important influencing factor is your attitude. If you expect the worst and are resistant to change, then you will spend a time similar to the Israelites wandering in the wilderness while suffering a slow termination of those once-great possibilities.

> *And whatever you do, in word or deed, do everything in the name of the Lord Jesus, giving thanks to God the Father through him.*
>
> — *COLOSSIANS 3:17 (ESV)*

Adopting an attitude of gratitude helps ensure you remain on track and on time to emerge fully armored and imparted with an anointing from God that is primed for activation. This should be your encouragement to pursue a posture of thriving even though circumstances may seem daunting.

This is the time for serious change, so embracing it with an open heart might just minimize the trial. Don't forget that the Israelites were literally on the physical border of crossing into the Promised Land, and their defiant, negative dispositions got them another forty years until only Caleb and Joshua remained from the original tribes to enter. Why? Those two had positive attitudes; the others, not so much.

OBEDIENCE

A big part of why we find ourselves in cycles of obscurity is thanks in part to our stubborn resistance to God's will and authority. Yes, we do have free will (Genesis 2:16–17) to choose Him or even to reject Him, but once we freely choose to accept God into our lives by inviting His Son, Jesus Christ, to be our Lord and Savior, we are encouraged to lovingly surrender our carnal will for God's sanctifying justification.

> *And Samuel said, "Has the Lord as great delight in burnt offerings and sacrifices, as in obeying the voice of the Lord? Behold, to obey is better than sacrifice, and to listen than the fat of rams."*
>
> — *1 SAMUEL 15:22 (ESV)*

The typical Western response to the subject of obedience is one of resistance because of a connotation to defeatism or subjugation. It stems from our cultural DNA implanted with a history of epic struggles to gain independence along with going around the globe to help ensure it for oppressed nations and states. But this battle is not fought with guns and tanks. Our most significant wars are fought in the supernatural realm where obedience is as desirable a characteristic in obscurity as it is for our military in battle.

It was your obedience to God's calling that first led you into this season. Maybe it wasn't the time you selected or even wanted, but there was a divine alignment waiting for you to simply show a willingness to heed His call through an obedient act. Do not abandon your willingness to obey God's prompting through the Holy Spirit. He is your guide in this life, and your open obedience to His relationship is key to walking with you into your new anointing.

CHARACTER DEVELOPMENT

Can we agree that as awesome as you are, there is still room for improvement? While some friends might say you have lots of room to improve, what is important is that there is room. How much or little is best defined by God. Thriving in obscurity involves a huge emphasis on character development. Note that we did not say huge development, but a huge emphasis. Why? Because our character defines who we are, how we behave, and who we most desire to be.

Before God can gift you with a new identity in Christ, He first must lead you to break free from your enslaved character mentality. Consider what it is to which you are a slave. Is it work, money, golf, pornography, fear, adultery, alcohol, or lack of forgiveness, to name a few? Similar to the Israelites who were not yet ready to receive God's gift to live as free people in the Promised Land until they had shed themselves of their captivity character, He cannot bless you until you too are delivered. Developing your Christ-character sets a solid foundation upon which God begins building a new, improved you.

A few tips to help you pursue the character God desires to develop in you is to remain humble, live out your faith walk, be purposeful in your actions and decisions, practice being self-disciplined, and focus on holding yourself accountable for your actions and inactions.

DISCOVERING SELF

There is really nothing more destructive than fooling yourself. It is understandable if you are simply unaware or misinformed, but to know better and fail to do better is a really self-destructive position within which to operate. Paul's warning in his letter to the communities in Galatia nails it on the head.

> *For if anyone thinks he is something, when he is nothing, he deceives himself.*

> — *GALATIANS 6:3 (ESV)*

One of the biggest stumbling blocks we face while trying to scramble out of our wilderness is deception. When self-actualization is directed by your own definition of what is considered the sanctified person as opposed to the revelation from God, we teeter on a form of idolatry.

"I'm this" and "I'm that," self-expressions limit God from showing us who it is we actually are. When we remain inward looking, we only see who it is we want to believe we were. Even if that is a lie. But looking up allows us to see God's reflection and thus the standard by which we may compare the Christ in us to who we know the true character of Christ to be.

We will never be the perfect manifestation of Christ, but through the sanctification process of our faith walk to mirror Jesus, we may begin to travel in His light of justification. It is within that stream of living for and like Christ that we begin to identify who it is we actually have become. Rising to the level of thriving requires a new identity and a new name as assigned by Jesus Christ.

> *I will give in my house and within my walls a monument and a name better than sons and daughters; I will give them an everlasting name that shall not be cut off.*

> — *ISAIAH 56:5 (ESV)*

DIVINE ALIGNMENTS

There's a popular sociological theory called, "Who's in Your Five?" It proposes that you are an aggregate of the five people closest to you. We like the saying, "Show us your friends, and we'll show you your future." It is the very same concept. Want to be a success, then hang out with successful people. Want to end up divorced, then hang out with single and divorced people. There is truth to the old adage, birds of a feather flock together.

Moving into obscurity is often marked by the loss or absence of people we feel are the closest to us. In addition to a separation from family, the desperate sensation of being alone creates a panic effect that sometimes drives us back into the arms of old, destructive relationships. Do you recall what the newly liberated Israelites said to Moses? Yep, they wanted to head right back beneath the crushing oppression of Pharaoh's dominating fist.

We can assure you that until you first learn to become a true friend *to* others that you will never become a true friend *with* others. It is in the fire of obscurity that we see the shallow, surface-level acquaintances consumed like a flash in the pan. It was many of those loose connections that prevented you from establishing solid connections with fellow believers. Why? Because bad seeds corrupt good company.

Do not be misled: "Bad company corrupts good character"

— 1 CORINTHIANS 15:33 (NIV)

One of the markers that you are thriving in this season and the end is in sight is that you will become open to new relationships. These connections go deeper than acquaintances based on hobbies or work in common. Instant connections with others are called divine alignments. They are the people God placed in your life long before you would have ever imagined meeting them. And they, like you, recognize the spiritual significance of the friendship.

Another sign that you are thriving and progressing is the connection to mentors and/or a spiritual mother or father. These divine alignments are often provided by God as someone to walk you through the rest of your journey or usher you into the new season.

Let us look back to Moses. Although he was raised in the pharaoh's palace as a prince, the truth was, he had been separated from his biological father. Part of Moses's obscurity challenge after fleeing Egypt following the murder of a taskmaster was allowing him to liberate himself from the chains of a dysfunctional childhood. As he neared the end of his own forty years spent as a shepherd, he not only experienced his God encounter at the burning bush, but his father-in-law, Jethro, assumed the role of his spiritual father.

When Moses shared of his God encounter and his ministry of leading his people to freedom from Egyptian captivity, Jethro affirmed his calling and supported him.

> Then Moses went back to Jethro his father-in-law and said to him, "Let me return to my own people in Egypt to see if any of them are still alive." Jethro said, "Go, and I wish you well."
>
> — EXODUS 4:18 (NIV)

This is how you may identify your spiritual mentor and know you are on the right path toward the activation of your new anointing. Mentors are there for you as appointed by God, and like Jethro share these characteristics:

- Listens without judging.
- Affirms and praises God for the work He has done and is doing in your life.
- Speaks the truth even when it's uncomfortable.
- Helps you create an action plan that is best for you and those you serve.

SPIRITUAL PRIORITIZATION

The best illustration for explaining this marker for success in obscurity is to consider your favorite hobby or activity. Did it take precedence over attending church services or faith activities? If so, then obviously playing golf instead of attending worship services meant your priorities were self-aligned.

> But seek first the kingdom of God and his righteousness, and all these things will be added to you.

> — MATTHEW 6:33 (ESV)

The sense of abandonment and loss of most everything you once considered vital during your wilderness season is meant to help you focus on realigning what is truly important in your life. Part of that reprioritization is to make sure you are ready and capable of receiving the new spiritual gifts God has waiting for you. Leading you into music ministry when you would still rather spend your Sunday mornings fishing on the lake is not a position God will endure.

This section really does not require lots of explanation. It is based on Matthew 6:21 and once you develop the sincerest desire to spend time with God is when you know that you are moving wonderfully along in your journey.

> For where your treasure is, there your heart will be also.

> — MATTHEW 6:21 (NIV)

GROWING ROOTS AND DEEPENING WATERS

Remember when you first thought that the new job or promotion with a big fat raise meant that you had made it, or that maternity leave was going to be spent not worrying about keeping your position at the company? Now, recall the panic when you realized that all of what you thought you had so carefully laid out in life began to completely fall apart?

Experiences like these usually occur at your launch into obscurity and can resurface in various forms along the way. The reality is, we were never once promised a pampered life as a follower of Christ. If you assumed that living the blessed life meant champagne and caviar, then you assumed wrong. Need evidence? Take a look at how Jesus and most of His disciples died.

Modern crucifixion aside, we have and will face persecution in this life. In addition to that persecution, hard times and occasions we may protest as not being fair will remain a constant in our life. The difference comes not in the circumstances we endure, but in our response. What were sheer panic or anxiety reactions to traumatic situations in the beginning of our renewal journey, become less of an attack and more of an opportunity to hand it over to God. Learning to wait patiently on the Lord is a sure sign that you are beginning to thrive in obscurity.

The less you worry and the more you pray is a significant marker along your path. Accepting that horrible things happen to good people is a reality we face. But whether you are facing financial calamity or a strained marriage, you will not abandon the power of prayer in a self-centered attempt to fix it yourself.

Winds will blow across the plains and the waters, but while the surface tension may be rippled or a leaf or two flutter to the ground, what holds us in place, in the presence of God almighty is the depth of our faith as rooted in Him.

> *Be still and know that I am God; I will be exalted among the nations, I will be exalted in the earth!*
>
> — *PSALM 46:10 (NKJV)*

ADAM'S BREAKOUT

MINIMIZE

Our first lesson before we could imagine thriving was learning how to minimize. In south Louisiana, we call it "cut bait." There is a reason the airlines limit the amount of baggage you can carry onto their flights. We should do the same thing in life.

When you are flying high in a season that we call success, you don't realize how much extra baggage you take on. Extra commitments, unneeded financial burdens, unfruitful relationships, and so many things that made you busy, yet are not necessarily productive.

In our last season of obscurity, we decided to downsize our home, we pulled the kids from high-tuition private schools and enrolled them in fine, free public schools, we passed on the fancy vehicle upgrades, and we cut our eating-out budget in half. We also focused on assessing and redefining every relationship and commitment. You may not want to hear this, but we actually cut out some relationships. It's what we call *pruning*.

Sometimes you have to recognize what is a "sucker branch." They might look good, but the truth is, they will never produce good fruit, and you should simply cut them off. Minimizing our lives helped us depressurize and prioritize what moments were most important in our lives. Jesus actually speaks to this.

> *And again, I say to you, it is easier for a camel to go through the eye of a needle than for a rich man to enter the kingdom of God.*
>
> — *MATTHEW 19:24 (NKJV)*

In biblical times, they didn't have eighteen-wheelers to transport goods from city to city. Instead, they had camels and other pack animals. Each day as the sun began setting, the gates of cities would be closed and locked down to protect against bands of raiders attacking under the darkness of night. If someone transporting goods arrived after the gates had closed, they were redirected to a small, single, heavily guarded door named "the eye of a needle."

All packages and goods would have to be unloaded from the pack animal and carried through the small opening by hand. The larger pack animals like camels would have to be completely unloaded then forced to crawl on their knees in order to fit through the doorway. The entire process was absolutely miserable for all involved. Jesus uses this imagery to help us identify how much stuff is burdening us down and potentially keeping us from entering into what really matters. You want to thrive in obscurity? Then lighten the load.

EDUCATE

The second, and possibly the most daunting, thing we learned to do for entering into a transitional season of thriving was to educate ourselves. By my mid-twenties I was an extremely successful youth minister. I levied that experience and education to coach others around the nation. By my early thirties, I had to learn how to start and thrive in a missional parachurch organization. Those years tossed me head-first into a trying process called *transition*.

It was with that major life change that we accepted an offer for directing a Bible school. Obviously, as a youth pastor I had no experience in that environment, but I was confident and courageous despite the steep learning curve. The transitions over each decade and into my forties showed a pattern in my life. Before I experienced a breakthrough, there was a wilderness season where obscurity helped refine who I was going to become.

Still, in my forties I mistakenly thought that God had put me through enough of these cycles and that we would remain comfortably on flat, solid ground for the rest of our lives. Many people have heard that saying "If you want to hear God laugh, tell Him the plans you have for your life." I guess He had a good laugh because there were more seasons of obscurity ahead. Why? Because God still had plans for us, and He needed to activate within us what it would take to succeed in those plans.

God's next plan was to have us start a church from scratch with zero resources. Like, actually zero resources. Honestly, by this time, I was tired of being educated. My frustration really boiled over when I sat in a gathering of church planters and none of them were over twenty-seven years old. Every one of them was fit and ready to go. Their ideas were fresh and creative. Each of them were social media gurus and I was still trying to figure out why Instagram was better than Twitter. How did I become dated overnight?

It is like the one middle-aged IT director told me, "I've been an expert nine times." You would think that by now that I had earned enough points to put God's calling on cruise control and bask in being honored for my wisdom and experience. Surely, I had worked and invested deep enough into the kingdom to sit back and enjoy withdrawing accolades of dividends from past investments.

This weak entitlement ideology is what obscurity sets you free from. Lay down your pride. Stop looking for validation for past accomplishments. Start asking questions. Turn on your learner and go educate yourself. Let new passions form. Rethink how you learn. Embrace the fact that someone half your age may be exactly who you need to listen to sometimes. Throw safety to the wind and LIVE!

SCOTT'S BREAKOUT

ONE OF THE greatest giftings God placed in my heart during my obscurity season was compassion. I will confess that I was never a compassionate person. There is a personality assessment called Strength Finders. It identifies your top thirty-five personality characteristics and ranks them in order of prominence. The goal of finding your strengths is to focus on the top five. I wasn't shocked to see the results of my test that listed Empathy (compassion) as number thirty-five.

I was not content to accept that I was more focused on achievement than caring for others, and of course, it would take a supernatural gift to address that deficiency. During my wilderness journey I began to sense a heart for men's ministry. I knew God had a work in mind to help set other men free from the chains of their past pain, shame, and guilt. Men in general were failing God, their wives, their kids, and friends. God set a path in my life for doing for others what He had done for me—build a better man. It would become the benchmark of my thriving in obscurity.

Men have been under the gun since...well, since the very beginning. So what are our options? The only true option is to move forward toward building a better man. But throughout time, men have amassed personal pain along with their earthly accomplishments. A big part of manhood is silently enduring the hurt as a wayward medal of valor. It has left us wounded, more fragile than we would ever acknowledge, in an unwelcome transition of gender roles, and unsure where to seek the healing light of restoration.

I had manhood all figured out. Conquer—Claim—Repeat. It was my method, but more so, it was my madness. Driven by a desire to push and occupy every empty space in my life, an addiction for consumption became more powerful than my desire to pursue Christ. Consumption of earthly accolades became vital in helping me medicate the wounds of manhood and the self-inflicted injuries carried in silence as a price for being a man. It is easy to get wrapped up in a defeatist demeanor. Our culture's latest liberal tag of toxic masculinity has guys laying low on the high-fives and grooming their lumberjack beards daily. God did not design us to conform to something we are not. He also gave us a very simple blueprint on how to actually be a man.

> *Watch, stand fast in the faith, be brave, be strong. Let all that you do be done with love.*
>
> — *1 CORINTHIANS 16:13–14 (NKJV)*

We were made in His image, and that image is perfect by design. God's intention, creation, and calling for man was not meant to be compromised, watered-down, or neutered so androgyny is the new manly standard. But hold on, cavemen. This is not a call for us to reunite just yet. But it was a look at who we are called to be, and what we have become. When did this social shift occur, where were the godly men before us, and why is it important for us to pursue God's desire for our lives?

Men have no superior predator on earth, so we self-destruct at our own expense. God gave us dominion over everything. Why do we work so hard to change it, fix it, conquer it, or destroy it?

> *Then God said, "Let us make man in our image, after our likeness. And let them have dominion over the fish of the sea and over the birds of the heavens and over the livestock and over all the earth and over every creeping thing that creeps on the earth."*
>
> — *GENESIS 1:26*

When I think of the prototypical male, it is mind-blowing to consider Adam was only one step removed from God's likeness. Even the angels mistook Adam for the Father. In my mind, Adam would look like Dwayne "the Rock" Johnson. But despite the closeness of their relationship, Adam fell victim to the same thing we fall to every day—sin.

The question I have asked myself often, especially in the midst of my sin and pain, is, "If Adam couldn't hold it together, how can I?" You see, Adam was close, but no matter how his image reflected the likeness of the Creator, he was still just Adam. We can't rest in the reflection. We have to press into His presence. When we press is when we thrive.

While we should strive to be Godlike, we will never actually be God. Although, many men set themselves on a pedestal so that at the center of their own universe, they become god (very little letter "g"). That is called idolatry and does not go over well with God. Lucifer tried, and it did not work out too well for him and a third of the angels.

Sin has separated us from God. It is because of sin that pain evolves, and it is because of pain that our desire to soothe the hurting becomes our pursuit. And yes, even our downfall. But there is hope. Men were not called to be failures or flukes. We are ordained to serve as the head of our household and mirror the very image of God. There is a better path than lugging around the failures of our past.

God promises a better way, and there is actually more to this life than sports scores and hunting.

> *"For I know the plans I have for you," declares the Lord, "plans to prosper you and not to harm you, plans to give you hope and a future."*
>
> *— JEREMIAH 29:11*

Our mission must be to help mentor men who have fallen out of "church." I'm talking about the church as the body of Christ, and also the institutionalized worship. But mostly the body of believers; that is where the true church lies, and real change occurs. Many religions no longer feed the masculine soul of a man. Why? Because the shift toward single moms and grandparents raising their progeny has tilted the church's focus toward our wonderful sisters.

It wasn't their choice—it was our absence.

We must create change within the faith-based community for establishing processes to hold men accountable in a respectful way that shows them what honor and sacrifice look like in tangible examples. I love motivational posters, but what do they look like in real life other than a majestic image with cool font on glossy paper?

Men are suffering at the grips of drugs, pornography, alcohol, sex, and violent abuse. Silent suffering is not only destroying each generation of men, but also our national fabric. Men can reclaim their position as anointed by God. But we must first return to God through Jesus. There is no light without the Son. When we drop the dude 'tude and come to Christ, we will be restored in ways that Adam never knew. We are meant for so much more. We can proclaim the victory in Christ if only we will allow Him to fight the battle. This is a promise straight from God. Claim this promise!

> *And hath made us kings and priests unto God and his Father; to him be glory and dominion for ever and ever. Amen.*
>
> — *REVELATION 1:6*

And, as if we men have not had a rough enough go at it, we now find ourselves isolated from other men. Or at least the godly brothers who hold us accountable so that we can thrive in even the worst times. Can you name your top five friends? No family members, just friends. Why five? If I were a betting man, I would guess like me, you could not do it unless you are still in your twenties.

In our early years we are known by the number of our friends. But as we mature, we ground our identity in titles, degrees, promotions, or being parents. Yep, to no surprise, we become known by our accomplishments and kids. A study showed that the number of close friends people had in 1985 was three, while by 2004 it was zero. The number of people without any close friends in 1985 was 36 percent, and in 2004 it was 53.4 percent

A 2017 study showed most men had just one close friend. Of course, jobs and families play a role, but we men still see ourselves as singular in nature and without a need for close bonds or the intimacy of friendship. This is not the biblical standard for men. God created us for relationship—with Him and with each other. Good friends challenge us and call us on the junk in our lives. They care less about our salary and more about our souls.

Faithful are the wounds of a friend; profuse are the kisses of an enemy.

— *PROVERBS 27:6*

I know it is tough to reach out to make friends as we get set into our adult lives, but you are not alone. Even the churches are filled with friendless men just hoping to make a connection that will breathe life back into them. Be a man and start building your brotherhood. The next time someone offers to grab lunch or a coffee, take them up on it. Add to your five and add to the quality of your life.

As iron sharpens iron, so one man sharpens another.

Proverbs 27:17

9

POST-OBSCURITY AND THE NEW YOU

ARE YOU READY TO CELEBRATE? Sometimes exiting obscurity is like getting a new hairstyle and first seeing yourself in the mirror once the bib is pulled off. You mostly like what you see, but you are still not sure what has changed or how to maintain it at home. Although the apostle Peter and haircuts do not seem to connect, we want to slow-walk you through your first peeks of light in post-obscurity.

We identify with the apostle Peter on so many levels. He is kind of the disciple of the people in the way that most of us respond as he did. Peter was the unpredictable wildcard in the group who would speak with the mind of the Father in one moment and then be rebuked for saying something with Satan's influence the next. If Peter was anything at all, he was honest in his words and actions. Now that did not always make him right or popular, but the man wore his passion and impetuousness on his sleeve.

Now that you can begin to look back at your season of obscurity with a different perspective afforded through objective distance, try to identify the times where Jesus connected with you in the same ways He connected with Peter. During your trial, Jesus called you into a deeper relationship with God by teaching you, disciplining you, never abandoning or rejecting you. Although it may have been a wash of emotions in your season, your exodus will help you see what actually occurred more clearly.

Did you get muddy in the mix? We sure did, but that is part of the wilderness learning process. Not to pick on Peter, but there are at least thirteen times he messed up along his path to becoming the rock upon which the church was built (Matthew 16:18). And guess what? God never rejected Peter, because his stumbles were just like ours. They were opportunities for God the Father to lift us up and brush us off. Let us take a quick look at those times where God drew close to Peter:

1. Matthew 15:16 – Peter fails to understand the parable of the four soils.
2. Matthew 16:1 – Peter misunderstands Jesus's meaning about the yeast of the Pharisees and Sadducees.
3. Mark 10:13 – Peter tries to keep the children away from Jesus.
4. Matthew 14:22 – Peter fails to continue his walk on water.
5. Luke 22:24 – Peter argues with others about which disciple is the greatest.
6. Mark 9:5 – Peter interrupts the Mount of Transfiguration moment.
7. Matthew 17:24 – Peter speaks for Jesus without consulting Him.
8. Matthew 16:23 – Peter is rebuked by Jesus with, "Get behind me, Satan."
9. John 13:8 – Peter refuses to allow Jesus to wash his feet.
10. Matthew 26:41 – Peter falls asleep in the garden of Gethsemane.
11. Matthew 26:74 – Peter denies Jesus three time before the rooster crows.
12. John 21 – Peter quit the apostolic team and went back to his old job of fishing.
13. Galatians 2:11 – Peter distances himself from Paul and the Gentiles in fear.

(Reference – The 13 Failures of Peter! Jesus loves imperfect people.)

Isn't this an incredible list of what some see as mistakes, yet we now know were lessons learned as intimately taught by God? Each opportunity for growth empowered transformational change. How else could you explain Peter's trajectory from once cowering to a little girl when he was asked if knew Jesus, to becoming the emboldened leader we find in the Book of Acts? Talk about change!

Our emphasis in this chapter is revealing to you that what we see in Peter's pathway is a roadmap you can follow for activating the new anointing despite whatever you may have experienced in your past. God has given you a new name and identity, and now it is your choice to claim and activate it. As you step into the light of your fresh anointing, be aware you are still learning to apply new giftings in the same old environment from which you briefly disappeared. For some (maybe most) people it is like a fawn taking its first steps on long, wobbly legs.

While it won't be long until that baby deer is darting through the forest as a masterful buck with wicked-keen senses, your emergence into a new life phase requires perseverance. While God has imparted His new gifts within you, there remains a process for becoming aware of what those gifts are and exactly how God wants them to be used for the kingdom.

The best ways to identify what gifts God gave you and how those gifts are to be applied in your daily life is to continue reading His Word daily, pressing into your prayer life, connecting yourself to people who support and affirm your faith walk, and remaining sensitive to the direction of the Holy Spirit.

In this atmosphere you will begin to reap the benefits of having progressed through your season of obscurity. Some of those benefits are:

1. The revelation of who you are.
2. The assurance of whose you are.
3. The identification of personal and spiritual blind spots you were not aware of.
4. The identification of strengths you already possessed but did not realize.
5. The true condition of your heart, character, and faith.
6. The maturation of your walk with Christ.
7. The anointing of supernatural gifts.

8. The trial-by-fire confidence leading to closer fellowship with God.
9. The death of ourselves for gaining a new beginning in Christ.
10. The ability to discern God's voice as well as Satan's deceptive call.

NEGATIVE RESULTS

Earlier we discussed the importance of choices. Exiting your wilderness season does not necessarily mean there is a ticker-tape celebration waiting for the new, positive you. Through our choices and negative attitudes about transformation, it is possible to emerge from this supernatural renovation opportunity feeling further away from God, more self-centered, and encased in a spirit of cynicism.

It's possible for us to come out of the wilderness but for the wilderness to remain in us. Rob Renfroe

(CREDIT – *A Way Through the Wilderness: Growing in Faith When Life Is Hard*)

> *Be careful. …Make sure that your own hearts are not evil and unbelieving, turning you away from the living God.*
>
> — *HEBREWS 3:12*

Why, when, and how you exit from within obscurity depends heavily on the way you embrace the COST of the season. The calling, obscurity, stabilization, and transformation are all opportunities given to you as choices to follow Christ into a posture of sanctification through the purification fires of your wilderness season. It is never too late to embrace what it was you went through. Jesus is waiting for you!

POSITIVE POTENTIAL

We have identified four positive traits that may be gained during your wilderness season. If you have remained persistent through the journey, these life lessons will exponentially increase the gifts God has imparted within you.

1. Dependence.

God does not need your praise, but He does desire your relationship. Stubborn, self-reliant independence may have been worthy of chest-pounding prior to your trial, but that is not where God wants you to be, nor is that behavior conducive to a sacrificial relationship. Actually, without breaking the chains of self, God cannot use us no matter the gifts we may possess. Leaning into the presence of God shows a strength of character that speaks to your willingness to surrender self in exchange for His glorification.

2. Purpose.

Although you have recently walked out of a season where purpose eluded you, it is now time to see clearly. Part of that new vision will show you the purpose for having experienced that latest season of obscurity. Epiphany moments start painting the picture for filling in the gaps of what just happened. Instead of chaos, you become firm in the facts that there was a purpose for your trial and a purpose for your life. As your new anointing comes into view, you will also apply those new gifts to a fresh purpose for your service to the kingdom.

3. Patience.

Can you imagine if Moses decided to lead his people out of Egypt before his burning bush encounter with God? Or what if David decided he could not wait to activate his anointing as the future king of Israel? How about if Joseph chose not to wait to see his father and brothers and fled Egypt to find them? Just think of Elijah refusing to hide out until he was called again to serve. Think about a twelve-year-old Jesus crucified on the cross because He wanted His ministry to begin sooner. And do we really have to explain Job?

When examined through a spiritual lens, patience is much more than waiting. Enmeshed within patience are active virtues such as praying, serving, seeking, listening, sharing, doing, learning, trying, failing, loving, hurting, renewing, restoring, and resurrecting to name a few. Our season of obscurity put us through plenty, and it is not until we step out into the faithful light of Christ that we see patience meant so much more than doing nothing until God moved.

God never stopped moving while you were in your wilderness. As you grew to embrace patience, you were also adorned with the new gifts needed to move you out of that season and into an activation of your new identity's anointing.

4. Faith.

The irony is that faith led you into the season of obscurity, and it is faith that is the most difficult thing to hold on to during your trial. In order for you to intimately possess faith, it must be tested. Although we claim to have faith, it is only through the fire that it is either confirmed or killed. Faith was important during your obscurity and now it has been strengthened. It will serve you in pursuing your call to action in this new season of growth and service.

Growing our faith through testing and endurance allows us to persevere when it is easier to quit. Only when we endure by faith will we come to receive God's ultimate reward of equipping us to know perfect fulfillment and the joy of accomplishing His will.

COMMON QUESTIONS

1. How does obscurity influence major transitional seasons of life?

Obscurity is a major transitional period of life, but its intended purpose is to better prepare you for seasons outside of the wilderness walks. Times such as graduation, career changes, marriage, childbirth, retirement, empty nesting, death or loss of loved ones, and changes in financial stature are but a few examples of seasons where the activated anointing of God's gifts are imparted to sustain us.

2. How to identify the end of obscurity's season?

Seasons of obscurity are shrouded in uncertainty and questions about what it is that you have been plunged into. One tangible marker of the exodus is when you stop having to ask "Why?" and begin to appreciate the "Because."

3. How to conceptualize, memorialize, or document the season of obscurity?

The visceral emotions attached to your obscurity experience are very real and present, but just like most experiences in life, the intensity will fade. The sharpness of thoughts, worries, wonders, and miracles will dull as you move triumphantly into your new anointing. Once you gain a bit of clarity through objective distance, begin to journal everything (reference Adam's actual journaling in his breakout section as he was in the midst of a season). Journaling is a great tool for reminding yourself of where you have been as you will always appreciate where you are. It's also an incredible witnessing resource for others in their journey.

4. How to identify the new spiritual skill sets and apply them?

God blessed you with these gifts through the Holy Spirit, and completely opening yourself up to the Holy Spirit will reveal them to you. It is like reading an owner's manual. God knows how best to operate within those gifts, so He, through the Holy Spirit will show you how it is done. But you must be willing to open that manual. Discovering how to apply your gifts will also be revealed by the types of gifts received. Healing, the prophetic, intercessory prayers, and possessing a servant's heart for missions, to name a few, direct you into your areas of kingdom service.

5. How does obscurity affect spouse, family, and friends?

If those who know you do not see the light of transformational change, then they may not know you as well as first assumed. Because of the spirit-led nature of change, your spouse should be the primary beneficiary of your new anointing.

Our wives are our *ezers* (the Hebrew word for rescuer, helpmate, and strength) and they're our equals—two as one (Genesis 2:24).

As the most important person in your life next to Christ, your spouse will also experience the blessings of God's gifts to you. Please understand that never will a spouse be pulled apart from their other half because of the new identity. Supernatural change is God assigned and intended to improve upon what was currently in place.

Depending on the level of relationship with family, they will experience the new you, but will not also have the intimate benefit of relationship as a spouse does. As far as friends go, you may actually realize that some people you considered friends were only acquaintances or co-workers. It is vital to connect yourself with like-spirited people who fully invest in your anointing and service ministry.

6. How to properly communicate about obscurity?

Remain open to others in obscurity. Mentor when appropriate, but do not deny them the growth opportunities by short-circuiting their walk. You now have the benefit of having explored the depths of obscurity thanks to your struggles. Now is your opportunity to share those struggles so others may understand what it is they are going through minus the negative effects of confusion, chaos, and despair.

Using proper terms will help you and others frame your experience in an accurate context. Remember in the introduction that it was Adam using the term *obscurity* that lit the bulb for Scott's understanding of what it was that he had just experienced? You be the light for others by correctly communicating your experience.

ADAM'S BREAKOUT

Having cycled through obscurity multiple times, I have found some beautiful characteristics that emerged in me. First and foremost is patience. I can now recognize that God truly lives on a different time frame than I do. I have stopped pestering Jesus for what He has promised, and I have settled into the confidence that He will fulfill in me what He has promised in His time.

I have actually learned to let Jesus surprise me. If you are like me (a little controlling), then you hate surprises as well. But God is a good Father and He loves to surpass our expectations. He loves to surprise us!

Think about those YouTube videos of kids opening the box to find a puppy for their birthday, or the overseas-stationed military parent who shows up unexpectedly at the school pep rally. The elation of joy those kids experience is monumental. Our walk with Christ should be marked by monumental moments of elation in God's miracles that we did not see coming. I have learned to enjoy the surprises and to even look for them in everyday little things.

The other great characteristic that obscurity has developed in me is understanding. Understanding for others as they journey in and out of seasons of obscurity/dryness/wilderness. The old adage "You don't know what you don't know," is so true. I never understood why people often acted so defeated. I was notorious for telling people to "get up and do something great," not understanding that God was doing something great in them instead of through them in that moment.

Understanding is really the engine of kindness. Attempting to "walk a mile in that person's shoes" allows us to really see and understand the plight of others. That kind of understanding generates sincere kindness for others every time. And wasn't it Jesus's kindness that led all of us to repentance anyway (Romans 2:4)?

A bit of advice I would give to others that are coming out of dry times/obscurity is to enjoy the miracle. Reflect the light of the new dawn. Don't feel the need to qualify for others. I have often minimized the excitement of the new season because I did not want to discourage those that were still in obscurity.

In Romans 11:14 the apostle Paul uses this verbiage, "provoke them to jealousy" to set a truth into motion. He is speaking of the Jews who will not accept Jesus as their Messiah. Paul loves them dearly, and completely understands their position and logic because he used to be one of them. Instead of vilifying these Jews or even being frustrated with their stubbornness, he tells the Gentiles to shine forth all of the amazing miracles that Jesus is doing in their lives.

He relays that this will provoke these Jews to want what they have. When you come out of seasons of obscurity, tell the world how good your God is! Shout it from the roof tops! He has never forsaken you and He never will. There is a new you on the other side of obscurity and God is so excited for you to embrace it.

THIS IS a special addition to Adam's Breakout Session, as he shares an example of his journaling through one of his seasons of obscurity.

My Soul Aches

My Soul Aches and nothing brings reprieve.

I cannot discern if the Lord has abandoned me, or I Him. When I sit still, He does not come to me. When I busy myself with His business it does not prosper. There is no teaching that brings me solace. No minister that speaks hope to me. I am in the dark place. Failure dominates my thoughts. The past haunts me as I compare it to the present. I fear my time of usefulness is done.

I am surrounded by those awaiting my orders, but I have none for them. I am utterly beside myself. To act is to err, but to wait is to die. The Holy Word brings me only momentary comfort. I am not able to give myself wholeheartedly to the work, for I fear the direction unclear. I have tested many waters and none of them have resonated in my soul. I have been forced to lay down every treasure.

The past trophies are an embarrassment due to the present position. I am not content to sit at His feet as hard as I try. I am distracted by myself. In my brain I know this is some beautiful process, but if the goal is to make me more dependent on Him, then why are we so far away from each other? If the goal is to cleanse me unto a more righteous vessel then why am I more fleshly than I have ever been? If the goal is to impart into me some depth, then why am I so shallow?

Nothing is growing! Everything is dormant! The world is passing me by, and I am becoming a sluggard. What is being asked of me? Why have I been shelved? There is no strength in my arms. My mind fails me as one with Alzheimer's. And yet I have no desire to earnestly seek Him. I long for Him to revive me. My generation is confused by all the voices. I have faced my doubts and am more convinced now that Jesus is the only hope, but I have no voice for my generation. No place to even invite them to.

My studies are incomplete, my relationships are weak. My leadership is wanting, and my intimacy is lacking. Failure surrounds all the day. I fear to give up on visions of grandeur lest I settle into the place of common. Young men no longer look to me for direction, old men no longer seek me as a source to bring them relevance. I will not seek after the things of this world so I cannot bond with my peers.

I am the fad that ended, the toy from three seasons ago, the flip phone, skinny jeans, and tube TV. "Wasted," whispers the enemy in my ear. "While others were preparing for this season you were wasting your efforts for another's ministry." I fear I have not developed properly. I do not have the skills for this next season, yet I'm too far down the road to go back and get them. My Soul Aches.

There is a nagging desire to run away that must constantly be crucified. I at least know that when you are lost, do not leave the present spot, for if you are to be rescued you must not continue to wander deeper into the wilderness. Even the broken seem to prosper around me and it's all I can do to see them as a friend and not a foe. I will not compete! I will not compete!

I fear that all who have joined into partnership with me are doomed. I love them so much! So somehow to obtain to His likeness and the fellowship of His sufferings. This has been a long dark chapter. I thought if I surrendered position and prestige that I would be rewarded with presence and purity. Purity of motive, purity of ministry.

That real hurting people would be really delivered. Presence would be tangible. I do not sense you in our gatherings, I do not see confidence in the eyes of those around me nor do I find it in the mirror. That wretched mirror!! It lies so truthfully. It sees so earnestly but never offers hope. For hope has been dashed with every unresponsive effort. I have no strength to fight the forces that overwhelm.

I do not want the advice or counsel of Job's friends! Through every past trial, my hands held tight to yours, but now I feel no strength of touch. Anger desires to bubble in my soul like a pressurized volcano trying to erupt. "Abandoned you He has," cries my active flesh. But then buried deep in my soul, a faint pulse of faith seems to hint "He's here," and this causes the "Ache in my Soul." This ache is proof that I still must be coddled, that I am not the warrior that I portray from the platform. That foolishness is bound up still in the heart of this child.

So many love me. So many need me...that's the problem! My arms have never been stretched out far enough to save them...only one. I am plagued with the statement "well done, good and faithful servant." It haunts me in the night, and it frustrates me during the day. For the entrusted talent will not reproduce anymore.

I would climb, I would run, I would wait, I would speak, I would be silent, I would study, I would write, I would learn, I would go, I would stop, I would die, or I would live but none seem to be the right choice while all seem to be needed. I ache in my soul. Others are so busy being confident in their duties, yet I am unassigned. I can serve another, but you've said I was to lead. Then I will lead...but where do I lead? You gave me influence everywhere but where I am stationed? So then am I to serve that I may gain your influence so as to have the right to lead?

I have to be in the right spot for there are no other spots available. They have all been taken. The seats at the table are all filled yet I am still standing. Was I not invited to this party? Am I simply to wait on those seated? Why have we journeyed here? There is no life in death and there is no glory for you in my shame. You are the giver of life, so why does my Soul Ache? I can be content with serving if this is my place at the table, but there is no place at the table. You have groomed me to lead but there is no place at the table. If you would have me to stand then speak the words but everyone stares at me as if to say, "What are you to do?" The awkwardness is more than I can bear. Just speak! Just speak!

If you cannot trust me, then please remove me! My Soul Aches! I am shamed, for my small tribe looks to me for direction yet I have incurred your silence. The other tribes I have served will not even look in my direction as though I am unproven. I have become utterly undone. Where are you, Holy Spirit? Where have you led me or where have I dragged us? If it is a test then let me at it, if this be a punishment then let me endure it, if it be a development then may I develop through it. But not knowing is stealing my confidence.

My Soul Aches, for though you do not use me, I will not, I cannot, abandon us. Though there be no proof of your presence in me, I will not, I cannot, abandon us. Though failure seems to be the road I am to travel I will not, I cannot abandon us. Though I be the broken spot in this relationship I will not, I cannot abandon us.

For like Peter said, "Where else shall I go?" I have nowhere else. I know nothing else and you alone hold the words of life. And with this, my Soul continues to Ache.

SCOTT'S BREAKOUT

I want to use this space to share a few truths that have my heart feeling full and at a point of bursting with joy. If this were a basic training academy, I would salute you and congratulate you on a job well done. But the reality is, this is so much more than the completion of a course, a self-help book or a new certification. This is in the truest sense of the words, a new you.

It is doubtful whether God can bless a man greatly until He has hurt him deeply.

— A. W. TOZER

I know this to be true. I've been wounded deeply and blessed greatly by God. I've learned more about who I was created to be from the wounds. As for obscurity, it stunk. It hurt. It made me cry. It had me confessing to my wife that I was going to kill myself. It had me apologizing to our Christian counselor for being a bully. It had me making amends with my kids. It had me accepting the realities that I had been physically, verbally, and sexually abused in childhood. It forced me to accept that in my childhood I was a victim of violence and intimidation, and throughout my adulthood I relished violence and intimidation as a way to accomplish my job, control my relationships, and manipulate my way to the top of everything I wanted. It showed me that when it mattered most I was a grasshopper in the midst of giants. It showed me that I was not unfeeling, impenetrable, invincible, or unbreakable. Ultimately, it showed me who I was as a child of God. But you know what? Obscurity was incredible!

This is always the hardest part to pen. There is so much that goes into writing a book, that instead of the end being the end, it is actually a new beginning. I learn so much during the creative process and am overwhelmed through prayers and memories of my own time spent in obscurity. Despite the temptation to dwell on my past of struggles, I have been set free to rejoice in the victory of a new anointing. As part of those imparted gifts, I get the honor to share our understanding and hope with you as you traverse the wilderness path.

As I wrote each of my breakout sections, some took longer because the memories and emotions became too strong to simply write. That didn't mean I wasn't healed of it, it just meant I'm human and no longer have to hide the way I feel about what occurred before, during, and after my latest season. Remember, our past is only there to remind us, not to define us. This book is so personal to me that I am truly thankful you have allowed me to share it with you.

There are loved ones who might not immediately understand what it is you are going through, but they will definitely see the new inside of you. You will walk in the light of opportunities for moving into a healthy, intentional life where innumerable blessings await. And you will be a much happier person because of it because you have God's peace that surpasses all understanding.

This is a tough reality to face, so I pray you fully realize what you've just accomplished. It is not easy to look at ourselves without blinking or making excuses for who we were or what we did in the past. That is why these seasons of obscurity blur out the details of the past for helping you focus on a future God laid out before you. By progressing through this season of obscurity you have made a statement to you, and most importantly to God, that you will pursue and cling to Him throughout the transition. No one I know has become fully self-actualized without Jesus Christ as the lead in their life. Cling to the Rock.

And speaking of the Rock, I want to share my blessing with you. Jesus Christ has been so good to me, but hoarding the anointing oil in my jar is not fulfilling His calling to pour affirmation and life into others. I've been called to guide others into an understanding for God's wilderness seasons. I prayed over every chapter before I began to write, and I will continue to pray for everyone who has completed this book.

I am so fired up about what your future holds in store. This is my prayer for you:

Rak Chazak Amats!!!

The ancient Hebrew war cry encouraged God's warriors on to victory. It loosely means to be strong and of good courage, and to go forth without ever considering the possibility of defeat. Can you imagine living life with this stamped on your heart? No enemy too big, too strong, too intimidating. No calling of God too big, too bold, too demanding.

Joshua 1 tells about God's command to Joshua just before he leads the nation into the Promised Land. There were still enemies trying to occupy what God had promised, but He assured Joshua of his success and inspired him to not be afraid or discouraged. Instead, he was to remain strong and courageous because God was with him.

Have I not commanded you? Be strong and courageous. Do not be afraid; do not be discouraged, for the Lord your God will be with you wherever you go.

— *JOSHUA 1:9*

God is with you, and your Promised Land is a future blessing of basking within the light of God's will. Hero, nothing you have been through or are going through is unknown to God. It is not ever too hard, too tough, or too deep for God to rescue you. But, like Jesus says in Revelation 3:20:

> *Here I am! I stand at the door and knock. If anyone hears my voice and opens the door, I will come in and eat with that person, and they with me.*

Knock, call, or cry out to Jesus, and He is there with you. No pride. No ego. No shame. Only Victory. It is yours, if you are just willing to march forward with *Rak Chazak Amats*.

Well done. Now enjoy the victory and prepare to receive the gifts God has been waiting to share with you. It is going to be a blessed new season in your life, but if you begin to doubt or feel the old natural person trying to revisit the dark ways of former habits, just pat your palm across your beating heart and whisper:

"Rak Chazak Amats."
"Rak Chazak Amats."
"Rak Chazak Amats."

ACKNOWLEDGMENTS

We thank God for gifting us with this friendship. We knew it was a preordained connection and have both benefited from the sharpness of each other's iron.

Our wives are so incredible to have not only remained the steady hands during our respective wilderness seasons, but to have moved with grace through their own times of obscurity. We give honor and thanks to Adam's wife, Jami, and Scott's wife, Leah.

We give thanks for our children in hopes that they too will embrace the challenges lying ahead as they realize the unending promises of God. Adam's kids are Cohen, Moriah, and Addie. Scott's kids are Ava, Ellie, Max, Jamie, and Graham.

We want to thank the creative team at Five Stones Press for making this work their passion as well as ours. Cover design by Damonza, editing by Imogen Howson and Kendra Williams, and internal format and distribution by Five Stones Press.

PASTOR ADAM MCCAIN

Pastor Adam McCain is a passionate follower of Jesus Christ. Happily married to his college sweetheart, Jami, they have three amazing kids and serve as the lead pastors of Church on the Hill in Cedar Hill, Texas.

Adam began serving in full-time pastoral ministry at age nineteen, spending the first decade growing a revolutionary small groups-based youth ministry at a megachurch in Louisiana, where he and Jami first met. Today, they continue to support each other's callings, both Adam's teaching and preaching gift and Jami's skill for creating positive community change through her political influence.

After decades of being a headline speaker at national and international ministry events, Adam is best known for engaging audiences with his real-talk biblical wisdom and one-of-a-kind storytelling. Adam's calling is to raise up global leaders who are equipped to impact their communities by daily living out the doing-life-together and discipleship-making gospel of Jesus Christ.

In 2001, Adam became the director at Christ for the Nations Institute (CFNI). During the seven years of his directorship, the school experienced unprecedented growth and launched countless ministry leaders who are still serving churches around the world today. He continues to be a sought-after speaker there, including regularly teaching his course on personal discipleship.

In addition, Adam and Jami together provide mentorship and development to local pastors and their wives through the Global Ministers Network (GMN). From all ages and stages of life, Adam and Jami connect with these pastors regularly to encourage each other, share resources, and continue strengthening their skills in the challenging and rewarding work of leading people deeper with Jesus. Over the past ten years, Adam and Jami have mentored dozens of pastors who have reached thousands of people through their services and special events.

Since 2005, Adam and Jami have given their hearts to serving as the founding and lead pastors of Church on the Hill, a thriving small groups-based church centrally located in Cedar Hill, Texas, with a second campus in Mansfield, Texas. A significant number of the founding leaders they began with continue to serve in leadership even today—a testimony to the kind of lifestyle and lifelong pastoring the McCains champion and embody so well.

DR. SCOTT SILVERII

Dr. Scott Silverii is a son of the Living God. Thankful for the gift of his wife, Leah, they share seven kids, a French bulldog named Bacon and a micro-mini Goldendoodle named Biscuit.

A highly decorated, twenty-five-year law enforcement career promptly ended in retirement when God called Scott out of public service and into HIS service. The "Chief" admits that leading people to Christ is more exciting than the twelve years he spent undercover, sixteen years in SWAT, and five years as chief of police combined.

Scott has earned post-doctoral hours in a Doctor of Ministry degree in addition to a Master of Public Administration and a Ph.D. in Cultural Anthropology. Education and experience allow for a deeper under-standing in ministering to the wounded, as he worked to break free from his own past pain and abuse.

In 2016, Scott was led to plant a church. Exclusive to online ministry, Five Stones Church.Online was born out of the calling to combat the negative influences reigning over social media. Scott's alpha manhood model for heroes is defined by, "Be on your guard; stand firm in the faith; be courageous; be strong. Do everything in love." (1 Corinthians 16:13-14)